Games for Trainers
Volume 1

ANDY KIRBY

Gower

Published by
Gower Publishing Company Limited
Gower House
Croft Road
Aldershot
Hants GU11 3HR
England

Reprinted 1993

British Library Cataloguing in Publication Data
Kirby, Andy
    Games for trainers. Vol.1
    I. Title
    371.397

    ISBN 0–566–07260–2

Phototypeset by Intype, London
Printed in England by Clays Ltd, St Ives plc

GAMES FOR TRAINERS
Volume 1

Contents

Preface

I wrote this book because I needed it myself. Although there were a number of collections of training activities published, I found many too restricted to certain training topics (such as team building, leadership or management skills) for my needs, while others were out of print (Pfeiffer and Jones 1974–83), aimed mainly at particular groups such as drama students (Brandes 1982), school students (Bond 1988) or people with disabilities (Remocker and Storch 1979). I also found very little in them about the pros and cons of using games in the course room, the best way of using them and the problems which I might encounter. Finally, hardly any books were easily accessible by objective, which would allow me to take the learning points I wished to achieve and find a game that would help me to achieve them. It seemed to me that the notes I had made for my own use could be turned into something other people might find useful without much effort. This was my first mistake – it took a lot of effort!

My purpose in writing this book has been to share my enthusiasm for the use of games in the course room. Of course, games are not an answer to every course-room problem, but in this book I hope to overcome the preconception many people have, including some trainers, that games are alright if you are training something "soft" like self development or interpersonal skills, but that they should not be used on "hard" courses that aim to develop specific job-related abilities.

The Introduction sets out some observations and hints on the use of games, and some of the benefits and risks involved in using them. I have deliberately not addressed the ethical issues underlying some of the matters raised. The main section of the book is the 75 GAMES which are arranged in alphabetical order of title. They are presented in a standard format which sets out the Title, Summary, Objectives, Materials Needed, Timing Procedure, Commentary (on using the game in practice) and Variations. At the end of the book is an Index of Games by Objectives. Many of the games can be used to achieve more than one objective; this index will enable you to locate all the activities which might be used to explore a particular teaching point. Of course, some uses for particular games will occur to you that I haven't even considered. The book also contains an Appendix in the form of a programmed text designed to help trainers develop their own skills at devising and developing new training games.

Some of the 75 games described here will be old friends under new names, and I make no claim to have invented to majority of them from scratch. I have tried to tap that collective trainers' unconscious from which so many of our ideas and activities emerge, and to which we return them in an enriched form. What I have done is to codify a variety of the training games that I use, with some suggestions as to ways of using them to meet a variety of training needs. Even if you are familiar with the activity itself, however, you may find the way in which the structure has been described, some of the variations, or the training objectives worth reading. I would welcome correspondence from readers about variations they have tried to these games, thoughts they may have on the formulation of the games, and any new games they may wish to propose for inclusion in possible future editions. All such contributions will be acknowledged.

A second volume, containing a further 75 games, is also available.

Andy Kirby

Acknowledgements

I acknowledge the help of all the delegates and trainers who have encouraged me to devise, develop, improve and, on occasions, abandon games. Colleagues and former colleagues at Environment Training Services, the Lantern Trust, the Birkbeck College Centre for Extra-Mural Studies, the Mary Ward Centre and Roffey Park Management College have all contributed to my interest in and enthusiasm for games. I would particularly like to thank CarolAnn Ashton, Paula Bullock, Lucy Britton, Sue Dean, Alan Margolis, Alan Mumford, Clare Shaw and Martin Thompson. Sarah Boland's advice on an earlier version of the manuscript has been invaluable. Many of the games described in this book have origins unknown to me, and I offer my thanks to the unknown inventors of those activities. Malcolm Stern's editorial advice has made the preparation of my first book for publication considerably less painful and more productive than it might have otherwise been. Finally, I would like to acknowledge the patience of my lover Mick Harrison for suffering my preoccupation with this project over the past eighteen months.

AK

1

Introduction: The theory and practice of games

Active learning

The principle underlying the use of games in training is that participants learn better through doing than through reading, hearing or observing. This principle of *Discovery Learning* has become almost a commonplace in teaching and training (for example, Rogers 1989). In schools, colleges, universities and adult education institutions throughout the land, however, one can see passive learning methods being used for hours, even days on end. Admittedly, some of this is teaching rather than training. But in training of any kind – with its focus on behavioural and attitudinal change – active learning is definitely to be encouraged.

Participative training

I was brought up in the "Sorcerer's Apprentice" training environment, which remains the structure of much trainer training today. It worked as follows: you started as a "baby trainer" on information-based instructional training and, after serving your apprenticeship on this "bread and butter" training, you graduated to participative training. This required higher level facilitative skills and was therefore unsuited to the new trainer. Training games might be used sparingly by new trainers, but only under supervision, between consenting adults and behind locked doors. My experience has convinced me that the "whiteboard and waffle" mentality can fail at all levels of training, and that there is always room for participative methods. This is not to say that there can't be circumstances where a trainer needs to "tell". The layout of a letter, the procedure for staining a microscope specimen of human tissue, the principles of a staff appraisal system or the main channels of non-verbal communication may well be best conveyed by these means. Having said that, I *have* managed to cover the domestic arrangements on my courses by using buzz groups.

Participative methods are the most natural of all – they are the ones we use instinctively the moment that we are alone with a child. I do not therefore believe that there is any kind of training or teaching that cannot benefit from the use of games at some stage. Neither do I think that a particularly advanced level of trainer competence is required to use games as such. There is a wide range of games which make different demands on the trainer and the participants, and it will always be possible to find or devise one that is appropriate to the level of experience of the trainer and the amount of trust within the group. We have been brainwashed into a belief that participative training is for advanced trainers only, and I hope that this book goes some way towards dispelling that myth.

Games and their uses

Some writers on training have attempted to differentiate between types of game, simulation, puzzle and other activity work with groups (for example, Eitington 1989, Laird 1985). None of them, however, offer a satisfactory definition of games, so for the purposes of this book a training game can be defined as *a structured training activity with a content or process learning objective other than the completion of the activity itself.*

By the definition offered above, just about all outdoor training events can be regarded as games, as indeed they are. The focus of this book, however, is on structured course-room activities, therefore I shall not be much concerned with this type of outdoor training, although most of the activities described in this book could, be conducted in this way. Neither shall I be concerned here with the wide variety of detailed simulations which have been developed as training aids in a wide variety of situations. These really deserve a book of their own, and several have been written (such as Elgood 1984).

The essential characteristics of a game are that

(i) there is a learning goal;
(ii) there are clear definitions of what behaviour is and is not a

proper part of the activity, and what the consequences (payoffs) of those behaviours are;

(iii) there is an element of competition between participants (though there may be no scoring);

(iv) there is a high degree of interaction between at least some of the participants;

(v) the game has a definite end or point of closure;

(vi) and that in most cases there is a definite outcome (winners, losers, payoffs).

Such a functional approach ignores the equally important fact that games are fun, which is to say that carrying out the activity is itself motivating. Gesell (1946) pointed out that children do not have to be taught to play games, though as the Opies (1969) noted, they may have to be taught specific games. Indeed, children have to be taught to stop playing games. The intrinsic reward in game playing, however, is something that trainers can use in making training an enjoyable as well as a useful experience. But games do have particular functions: a trainer who simply places them into a session for the sake of it is not going to earn the involvement of participants or the respect of colleagues.

The advantages of games

So why use games? They have many advantages which you can use to sell them to managers, participants and training managers.

1. Anonymity

Less outgoing members of a group have the opportunity to participate in an active way without it being obvious to the others that they have made a decision to do so. This can be a confidence booster, and can encourage later participation in the discussion phase. In effect, participants model active involvement for themselves. The optional element, however, is important in allowing people the option of not participating if they so wish. (See **Contracts** below).

2. Developmental

For any given learning objective there are any number of games that differ in their complexity and in the demands that they make on the group. A trainer with a wide repertoire of games is going to be able to select the game that is most suitable not only to the needs of the group, but which also develops its abilities, and this will happen as

3

his or her confidence and experience grow. The use of training games therefore remains developmental for both participants and trainers. I would note here that a comprehensive stock of games also prevents the trainer from becoming bored by doing the same game time and time again, a boredom which inevitably reflects on the success of the activity.

3. Experiential

The source of learning is what the participants do rather than what they are told by the trainer. Above all, games are action-based learning, with all the advantages of that style of learning (outlined above). In particular, this can improve the memorability of the learning points.

4. Experimentation

Rather than talking about different ways of doing things, games offer an opportunity for participants to practice skills in a relatively safe environment, and to try out different options without risking the full consequences of doing so in the real world (much as a simulation offers a pilot the chance to practise crash landings without risking lives or expensive equipment). Sometimes this function games have of lifeskills simulation can be openly discussed with the group, but even if it is not it will still be important.

5. Flexibility

Games offer the trainer an opportunity to vary the conditions of the activity in accordance with the needs of a group, something that can often be difficult with more formal training methods. A game may well go on longer than the trainer first intended, be aborted or be varied in some way, and a good trainer will be able and willing to accommodate this. It also offers the trainer an opportunity to model his or her flexibility of approach while achieving the learning objective.

6. Full participation

The involvement of all group members becomes the norm in games. In many other trainer-centred activities the trainer interacts with one participant at a time, and this tends to be the most dominant fraction of the participants, whether in terms of co-operation or resistance. Games set up a requirement for full (and often equal) participation by each member. If each person has been seen to do something, then the less vocal or socially skilled members will be more encouraged to feed back both in the later stages of a game, and in discussions and other verbal activities further on in the course.

7. Group responsibility

A game gives a group the opportunity to take decisions for itself, and reduces dependency upon the trainer as the source of responsibility. The facilitative role of the trainer remains vital, but the group will have to establish its own principles and ways of abiding by them. In some cases (team-building) this can be a major objective of the course. In others it breaks down preconceptions of what learning and training are while also achieving other course objectives.

8. The learning cycle

Kolb (1984) and Honey and Mumford (1986) have independently developed models of learning as a cycle of four stages. They have argued that any effective learning event passes through all four of the stages of Action, Reflection, Theorizing and Planning for future occurrences of the same situation. The process of a game goes through all of these stages. Some trainers contend that training games appeal only to Activists – those people who have a high need for the first of these four stages. A well designed and executed training game, though, will cater for the needs of all: the Activist (who needs to be involved in an activity to learn), the Reflector (who needs to think about the experience afterwards), the Theorist (who needs to be able to work out the details of any underlying principles), and the Pragmatist (whose main concern is how to apply what has been learned). Figure 1 relates the stages of the game to the parts of the learning cycle.

9. Memorability

Perhaps because each game is unique in what it feels like to play, games tend to be memorable. This acts as an anchor that can help participants to recall what was learned (though there is a risk that they will recall the game but not the objective – like when you recall a commercial but not what it advertised).

10. Motivation

The "fun" element of games ensures that participants are motivated to take a full part. Some groups of participants who dislike any element of what they consider to be frivolity in a training course may be troubled by this. I find that an exercise has to be sold to such participants on the grounds of the usefulness of its learning

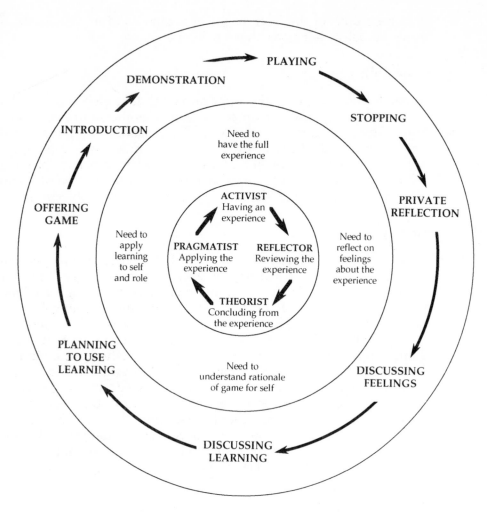

Figure 1. The learning cycle and game playing. Inner circle: learning cycles; middle circle: needs of learning styles; outer circle: stages of a game.

objectives. In general, though, the fun element encourages most participants. The competitive edge that exists or which can be perceived in some games is no doubt a motivating factor.

11. Multiple relevance

Although the trainer will have a reason for introducing a particular game, it may well be that participants will get something else out of it. The open nature of games and their (correct) processing ensures that what people actually gain from the game is fully expressed even if it is not what the trainer and his or her employers intended them to learn.

12. Payoff for all participants

Although there may be winners in the more competitive games, there is a payoff for all participants in terms of learning experience. It is also possible to organize the activity in such a way that there is no stigma for the losers.

13. Peer learning

Arising from this is the fact that most of the learning for a participant will come from his or her peers. This is a useful point to be able to make in the training room because it promotes networking, interdependence among participants and a tendency not to see the trainer as the source of right answers. Such a modelling effect (see p. 19) can be very significant, and in the long term can enable participants to considerably broaden their understanding of what a learning event can be.

14. Physicality

Most games operate by making a problem or a skill into a physical reality. Such a process can be a very powerful way of putting people in touch with their own feelings and reactions (**Fists** is a good example of this – assertiveness literally made flesh). By locating a problem or skill in their own physical space, participants are encouraged to become involved with it rather than treating it at an abstract intellectual level. This is a key to self-awareness (Clark and Fraser 1987).

15. Process issues

Participants are more likely to be their real selves in games than in many other sorts of training activity where they will conform to what they think of as the participant's role. They therefore demonstrate the way in which they react and interact in real life situations, which can itself be the subject of discussion (process intervention) at a later stage in the activity. This is particularly important in team-building work and any training where feelings are examined.

16. Rapidity of learning

Compared to unmanipulated experience the time frame of a game is very compressed, and the effect of this is to accelerate learning. This is an advantage of simulation learning methods, of which games can be seen as a special case (Stammers and Patrick 1975).

17. Realism

Even when it is not a simulation, a training game functionally represents some aspect of real life, thus making for ecological validity

– it examines the issues and skills of everyday experience in the language that that experience needs. A degree of reality is experienced that might not be possible with many other training methods. The feelings evoked and many of the responses generated will be very similar to those in the situation for which the training exercise is designed to prepare participants. By stressing these parallels between training and every day situations, games may help to promote the principles of continuous learning (Institute of Personnel Management 1984) with associated benefits for the individual and the workplace.

18. Risk taking

It is possible for participants to take risks in a relatively safe environment during games. Through contracting (see p. 16) the effects of loss of face are minimized, and risks can be taken which might seem too formidable in an ordinary environment. The atmosphere can remain supportive throughout.

19. Skill development

Many games require a degree of organizational skill which may not actually be the main objective of the game. The development of those skills, however, is an achievement that many participants will recognize.

Using new games

It is hard to use a game for the first time and trainers – like surgeons – can be unwilling to admit that they are piloting a game. One way around this – especially if you are part of a training community – is to hold an occasional "Games Laboratory". Each person brings a new game or activity which is played out, and then the trainer receives feedback on how it went. The others can either be asked to be themselves, or to role-play a target group from which real course participants are likely to be drawn. Feedback can be on the way in which the game was managed as well as its relevance to the teaching points (see below).

It is important to be fully briefed on the use of a game before attempting it. With some games, all the instructions are issued at the start, but with others some instructions are given as you proceed. Be clear on the stages and the variations of a game and any material you might need. Ask yourself questions like "How will I achieve the learning point if the game goes wrong?", "How will I deal with reluctant participants?", "How will I answer someone who wants to know why I am carrying out this game"? I witnessed a colleague of mine fall foul of this in using a game she liked but which was not really relevant to the particular course. When challenged to justify the game she could not do so (and neither could I). We both rightly had to work hard to restore our credibility for the rest of the course. You may even have to consider whether games are the most appropriate way of covering this learning point with this group. Trainers of a participative bent are often reluctant to concede that "tell" might be the best way of achieving some objectives.

Also, consider "bread and butter" questions such as the way in which you are going to allocate people to groups, the time that you have allowed for processing, whether and how you will advise the participants of time limits, and how you will manage to address process and content issues during de-briefing. Your handouts – particularly observers' checklists – might need customizing to meet the specific learning objectives of your course. Also be sure that you have everything that you need; equipment, furniture, copies of checklists and documentation where indicated, your briefing material, not forgetting a co-trainer if necessary. It is as possible in a training game, as it is in cooking for a dinner party, to discover half way through that you are missing a vital ingredient – and about as disastrous.

Keeping records of the precise way in which you run each course (mine is in index card form) is a useful way of developing variants of the games that you employ. The origin of this book was just such a system. I have found that participants themselves often have comments at the end of a course on how games could be improved, developed or used in more appropriate ways.

Another way of developing one's gaming is through co-training with a colleague on a course. This is a skill in itself, and is a very effective way to learn how someone uses games, since none of us can convey the full flavour of a training activity by describing it. There are some games in this book – energizers like **Exotic Fruits**, for example – which I refused to tell my colleagues about until I had a chance to demonstrate them at a Games Laboratory. In the same way that cooks often make mistakes in telling you their recipes, there is much that a colleague will not consider important enough to tell you about but which you will discover soon enough from working with him or her, and which might make the difference between a game being a failure or a success. The *Commentary* sections for each game serve just this function. Persuading your training organization that co-training in this way is money well spent is another matter! In fact, I find it easier to secure approval to co-train with people from other training organizations than from my own!

There may be some reluctance on the part of your training organization to accept games that you have devised yourself. Some training organizations regrettably do not encourage creativity, and value a game by how much it costs to buy. If this is a problem you may wish to suggest that one of your own games was learned from someone else; in the words of Dorothy Parker (1973):

If, with the literate I am
Impelled to try an epigram,
I never seek to take the credit;
We all assume that Oscar said it.

Feedback in games

I have already mentioned the offering and receipt of feedback several times, and it is relevant in all types of experiential learning to offer feedback (criticism) to participants on their performance. Many games require feedback to be given to each other by participants. Try to make sure that this is done sensitively and with an appreciation of why feedback is being given. I often clarify the following principles in the early stages of a course in which games are being used, some of which derive from Pfeiffer and Jones (1972):

1. Feedback should be offered, but can be refused. There is no point in giving feedback to someone who has not asked for it and doesn't want it. The best sign someone can give that he or she is willing to act on feedback received is the fact that they have asked for it.
2. Feedback should refer to *specific behaviours* where possible in particular situations.
3. The behaviour described should be modifiable. It doesn't matter how much feedback you give, it will have no effect if the person receiving it is unable to act on it. If someone's perceived eye contact is poor because they wear thick glasses, for example, it may not be helpful to comment on it.
4. The attitude of the person giving feedback must be positive towards the recipient. There should be no thought of scoring points from the person to whom you are giving feedback.
5. Feedback should take into account the relationship (for example, trainer–participant, trainer–trainer, participant–participant) between the giver and the receiver. It should meet the needs of the receiver rather than the giver.
6. Feedback should be well timed. There can be a tendency, particularly in interpersonal skills training, to withhold feedback until later. The ability of the receiver to recall feedback will have faded by then. On the other hand, people often want to

describe their own feelings about what they have done and other forms of self-feedback before they will be willing to receive anyone else's. Allow them to do this – they will benefit more from their self-criticism than from anything you might tell them.

7. Feedback should describe a behaviour rather than evaluate it: "When you raised your voice . . ." rather than "When you got all angry . . .".

8. Feedback should point out the consequences of a behaviour (e.g., "You raised your voice when you started speaking and that made me feel frightened about what you might do next."

9. "I liked it best when . . . because . . . I didn't like it when . . . because . . . Next time you might . . ." are good openings for feedback.

10. Feedback should be checked with the receiver and by others present. What is heard is often not what was intended. Asking the receiver to summarize the feedback also avoids the tendency for some people to ignore either positive or negative feedback.

11. Listening skills on the part of the receiver matter, and there are games in this book which examine that point (see Index). Not seeking to justify one's actions is particularly important.

12. Feedback through a third person (otherwise known as "gossip") is unreliable and ineffective.

A trainer may also seek – or receive without seeking – feedback on performance from either a participant or a co-trainer, and this should be accepted in the same spirit.

Types of game

I have yet to read a taxonomy of games, and therefore offer this brief guide to the main classes of game which are covered in this book.

- *Auction games* – where something is sold off for pretend money to members of the group. The auction process is often a part of a longer game, and is a good way of motivating participants and developing group identity. Strong non-verbal communication (such as getting the group members to all sit close together, "bringing them in" with hand movements) and enthusiasm from the trainer are required to make an auction game work. Seeing a few real auctions will give you some idea as to how to make it as realistic as possible.
- *Audience games* – part of the group serves as an audience for a few participants. The disadvantage of this is that the audience

part may become bored, but this is unlikely if they know that they are taking part in the discussion session afterwards or that they will get a turn to perform. Another disadvantage is that some people are frightened by the idea of standing up in front of a group. To minimize this, try and establish a degree of trust between the group members. Effective introductory exercises and a good contract (see p. 16) will help to establish this.

- *Chain games* – sometimes a participant will direct an activity to another person who will direct it again to a third. These chain games require a level of cohesion to have been established in the game.

- *Circle games* – for circle exercises, where people talk or carry out activities in turn, the trainer should demonstrate, and then ask for a volunteer who has the choice of which way the activity should pass. In this way, the "creeping death" to the last participant is a responsibility shared by group members.

- *Circle Centre games* – in circle exercises with one person in the middle, the trainer should start in the middle and be the one to be extracted first. Most of these games are energizers and attention switchers.

- *Exclusion games* – where one person has to be treated differently from the others in some way (for example, by being asked to leave the room while they decide on something). Since there is not time to (and little learning benefit in) repeating the game with each person in that role, then that person may feel excluded in some sense. These games should be used with caution and sensitivity, and some trainers are reluctant to use them at all.

- *Individual games* – each participant does something individually. The trainer should model the activity to start with.

- *Moulding games* – where one participant has the opportunity to mould, sculpt or order the group in some way. These are very good activities for team building where people can be physically confronted with the way that they are perceived by others. Their use entails an element of trust between group members, though. Another problem can be that everyone would like a turn, and that is clearly not possible. Hopkins (1981) analyses this type of game in more detail, and Benson (1987) offers advice on the use of these and other gestalt-based games.

- *Pairs games* – it is a good idea to encourage people to work with "someone you've worked with least". The involvement of the trainer may be necessary to make up the numbers, and so may his or her non-participation. Some trainers prefer to instruct group members as to who will work with whom. (I have known trainers agonize for hours over this. No wonder. If a group consists of n members and you want to divide them into groups of k people each, then the number of different possible combinations is

$$\frac{n!}{k!(n-k)!}$$

where $n!$ means $n(n-1)\,(n-2)\,(n-3)\ldots$ to 1 (for instance, $4! = 4\times3\times2\times1 = 24$). This means that games where you could run all the pairs possible (like **First Impressions** (p. 66)) can last a very long time. My feeling is that if people habitually work together on a course then this can be addressed openly as a process point in the group.

- *Relay games* – members of a team compete to all carry out an activity or a series of activities. They can encourage a high level of co-operation within the teams, but competition between teams may undermine good feelings within the whole group.
- *Swap games* – sometimes groups will complete a listing, writing or drawing activity, and the results will be acted upon in some way by another group (for example, **Challenge Challenge** p. 49). A good way to handle this is to give group members coloured discs with as many different colours as you want groups. Then give the groups coloured paper to work on with colours corresponding to the discs. The results can all be placed face down on the floor and group members asked to pick up any that are not of "their" colour.

Preparation

There are nine issues to be borne in mind in preparing to use games. These can be summarized as the "Nine As": Abilities, Age, Accommodation, Assailability, Assurance (safety), Attitudes, Authenticity, Actuals (Materials), and Anno Domini (Time).

Abilities and disabilities

Some of these games cannot be carried out with groups where individuals have certain disabilities, or will have different learning points where this is the case. It is the responsibility of the trainer to establish whether this will be a problem for the participant, and to do so outside the course room. Many of the games in this book require mobility, but the Objectives Index can be used to identify those where this will be less of a problem for the learning point to be established. Where members of a group have limited reading or writing skills, then the delivery of instructions may have to be made in some other form. In team work games, hearing and visual impairment proves to be less of a problem than in activities where participants are working on their own. A stock of double-size copies of handouts is useful to participants with limited vision. All this should not make many of the games in this book impossible, though some of them may have to be adapted.

There are also issues of health which might not immediately seem relevant to the ability to carry out the games in this book. I have known asthma attacks to be brought on by the unaccustomed activity of a training game. Participants may have other continuous or intermittent conditions which affect their ability to participate in the games, such as arthritis or even indigestion. Remocker and Storch (1979 p. 9) offer useful guidance on the conditions that are incompatible with certain types of game.

One way round this is to refer to item (iii) of the contract (below) which allows people to not participate without being questioned as to why they have decided not to. A condition such as those described above, however, may well prevent someone from taking part in most or all of the activities on a course unless they have been adapted, and I prefer to invite participants to discuss with me during the first break anything that might make it hard to participate in physically strenuous games. Make it clear that you have a full repertoire of other training activities available, and that they will not be stopping the group from learning anything.

The issue here is equality of opportunity – to which many training organizations and clients have a formal and public commitment. This means that nobody should be discriminated against in being selected to participate in an activity, or put at a systematic disadvantage while doing so. For this reason, specific genders and religious practices are referred to in this book only where they are relevant to the teaching points concerned (for example, equal opportunities).

Accommodation

Of course, there should be enough space to carry out the activity. Sometimes you will need a second or even a third room. You should know that you will not be disturbed, and it is a good idea to set in hand a system for leaving messages for course members, such as Post-It notes on the door, which does not disturb them during a game. This will also give peace of mind to participants. You may need to think about replacing glass doors, putting blinds or curtains over windows and sound proofing for some games. One room I used seemed quite isolated but proved to be positioned over an office whose occupants became rather disturbed by the noises emanating above their heads during an energetic round of **Whirlpool!** (p. 132). It is common courtesy to think of those around us who may be influenced by our training activities, and educate them in what we are doing and why we are doing it in a way which might seem to them rather eccentric.

Age range The activities are suitable to all ages, though presentation, prepared material and examples might have to be varied and take into account cultural differences relating to different age groups.

Assailability The level of risk that participants are being asked to undertake is very important. Always acknowledge that risk taking is involved, and thank participants afterwards for having agreed to such risk. The training contract will have a great influence on risk taking (see Pfeiffer 1973 for a further discussion).

Assurance (safety)

None of the games in this book require trainers to possess specific safety qualifications. Should safety issues be a concern to you (as they often are on outdoor training where many of these activities could be used), then Bank (1990) is a guide to good practice. Even so, excessive enthusiasm by some group members may lead them to forget the frailties of the other human bodies involved. One good way to prevent this from happening, particularly with physical activities, is to ask participants to remove their footwear. Another is to tackle the issue directly. In any case, all trainers should be familiar with basic first aid principles and practices, and they should know where to obtain expert assistance at all times. Some homework on the insurance provisions of your training organization and your legal responsibilities might not go amiss.

Attitudes Participants come to a course with attitudes and expectations. These will form the mini-culture of the course, which in turn will develop in a way that will promote or forbid games. I can think of some instructional courses where that culture made a game quite inappropriate. There is also the organizational culture (and that of the training centre) which may promote or oppose games. For some participants there will be cultural considerations of a more general kind. Some Muslim women, for example, would not feel able to participate in activities that involved physical contact with someone of the opposite sex.

Authenticity You must have a justification for using a game, and one that you are able to sell to your participants. Many games have multiple objectives, and the extent to which these can be met often depends on the nature and level of trainer intervention during the discussion stage.

Actuals Having all the materials to hand is vital. The credibility of the trainer is seriously undermined if he or she has to leave the room to do copying or to get some object needed for the activity. The materials needed are stated in the notes on each exercise, though.

Anno Domini

The timings given for the games are indicative only, and nothing has gone wrong if you take considerably less or more time than is suggested. The timings is this book are the shortest which I would find practicable, the variability occurring because the level of processing required and the length of the game will depend on the reason for which it is being used, the pattern of activities it is being used as a part of, and the composition and especially the size of the group. Sometimes it will be clear in a couple of minutes that all members of the group fully understand and can share their understanding of the game. Others may have to go through a long process of self-discovery. And a group that processes one game very efficiently may be painstaking on the next one. Don't forget that some trainers just work at a slower pace than others. It is important neither to compress nor extend the discussion, as this is the means by which learning and transfer of learning can be established and also gives the trainer useful information on the success of the game. I suggest you insert your own timings into the book.

Making games work

There are ten ways in which people can be encouraged to take part in games.

1. The group contract

A training session is a relationship between trainer and participants and, as in all relationships, ground rules will be established. An important way of encouraging people to participate fully is to reduce their anxiety; this can be done by letting them know what is going to happen, and what these ground rules are. To many experienced trainers this will be familiar, but it is worth rehearsing the aspects of these rules, or the *Training contracts* which apply particularly to games. These principles should be agreed at the start of the course, and should be open to renegotiation at any time during the course. It may seem rather artificial to go through this formally at the start of the course (and it is best deferred until after introductions and some warm-up work), but it is an important way of establishing an environment that is understood to be secure. The negotiation of the contract impresses participants with the fact that they are accepting a measure of responsibility for what happens in the course-room. One light-hearted way of doing this is to read a "Riot Act" (mine begins "no drugs, violence or exchange of body fluids in the course-room", and covers drinking, smoking and physical and sexual harassment), and then invite comment. Here are four issues that should appear in a contract:

(i) Confidentiality

The group should agree confidentiality:

(a) *within the course-room of what happens and what is divulged.* Although the main reason for this will be to encourage safe self-disclosure by participants, from time to time the trainer may well state or do things that he or she does not wish to have divulged (such as do what the delegates want even of it is not what his or her employer requires). There are also certain games with twists which should not be divulged outside the course-room. The trainer may wish to raise the issue of what should and could be said about the course in validation sheets, to line managers and to potential participants.

(b) *of the particular moment.* Participants should keep confidential what they are told by another participant at any time, without the consent of that person to divulge it to the rest of the group (including the trainer).

(c) *of reference.* During discussion sessions, participants may mention situations involving third persons who are known to some of the other participants. This is particularly likely on in-company courses. Confidentiality must either be established or participants encouraged to disguise any such references.

There are differences of opinion as to how overt confidentiality should be. Some trainers feel that with some groups confidentiality need not be openly discussed, but can be assumed; and I have worked with groups where the issue was never openly raised, but the level of self-disclosure and trust was such that I was sure that the delegates were quite happy that confidences would be respected. If there is any doubt, though, I prefer to openly discuss the issue of confidentiality.

(ii) Responsibility for using games

Members of a course should accept responsibility for using the course for self development and for the benefit of their organization; and

17

to realize that what they get out of an activity will depend on what they put into it. Trainers should realize that they do not have responsibility for the use to which learning is put by delegates.

(iii) Coercion

Participants will not be coerced into doing anything, and any participant should be able to withdraw from any activity at any time without being questioned about why they have done so: this applies particularly to any self-disclosure. What seems to be withdrawal is often a result of thought about some earlier activity that had particular meaning for an individual, and it is important that this process is not compromised. It may even be tiredness!

(iv) Clarification

Anyone who is unsure as to why a particular exercise was used can seek clarification from the trainer outside the main session of the course if appropriate.

2. Context

As a divinity student I learned that "a text out of context is a pretext": this applies to games. They should be firmly anchored in learning points which are relevant to the course, though when delegates learn other things and this emerges from the discussion of the exercise then this should be acknowledged.

3. Demonstrating

It is always useful for the trainer to demonstrate an exercise in front of the participants, both to model it ("I'm not asking you to do anything I haven't done") and to check understanding. In any case, some people respond better to a visual than an auditory stimulus, and these will understand better if they see something being demonstrated than if they hear the words. A demonstration involving other group members also begins the process of group participation.

4. Feedback

The way in which you give feedback is going to influence how threatened people feel by the idea of the exercise (see notes above on "feedback").

5. Natural justice

The terms on which a game are introduced are significant. A game should be *offered* by a trainer. In some cases, he or she will have to be deliberately vague about the learning point of the game, but it should never be forced upon the group.

6. **Pace**   The pace at which a game is taken should be appropriate to the group. A pause will often be necessary, for example, before feedback. After an energizer like **Whirlpool** (p. 132) the group will need to get its breath back. After **Good Grief** (p. 71) they will need to unwind.

7. Presentation

The way in which an exercise is presented is crucial. There are some group members – without having recourse to stereotypes I can say that I find some older and more traditional managers fall into this category – who will find the idea of "games" disconcerting, but who will quite happily accept a "management exercise" that is aimed at demonstrating a particular point. There is no need to ram your favoured vocabulary down the throats of your participants!

8. Receiving feedback

The willingness of the trainer to receive feedback will be an important feature in the group's willingness to accept his or her offer of further exercises. Modelling will also affect the ability of group members to accept feedback.

9. Timing

Setting time boundaries on an exercise can be very reassuring to group members. Whatever uncertainty they have over the game, they know that it will end at a definite time. Try and make the timer visible to them. I find a kitchen timer (with a magnet stuck on the back so I can fix it to the whiteboard) is ideal. In some circle exercises it is a good idea to be generous on timing for the first couple of rounds while participants became familiar with it.

10. Trainer modelling

The trainer cannot legitimately expect full participation from the group in an activity without fully taking part in it him or her self. At the same time, the trainer should not model a "correct" response. Modelling is a very powerful method of behaviour change. Psychologists have shown its influence on giving money to charity, crossing on a red light, encouraging violent behaviour in young children and helping drivers to change tyres (for instance, see Bryan and Test 1967, and Lefkowitz *et al.* 1955). For this reason it should be used with caution, though it is a strong factor in both content and process learning (see Anastasi 1979).

The stages of a game

Games divide into eleven logical stages: the offer, dividing the group, the introduction, the demonstration, the clarification, playing the game, observing the game, stopping playing the game, feelings, feedback/discussion and ending.

1. *The offer* – I have already stated that games should be offered to a group rather than being imposed. Usually this will include a statement as to why the game is being offered, but without mentioning the learning point. I often have to say something like "this game is about leadership, and you'll have a clearer idea of it when we've tried it out and discussed it." At this point raise any issues about the contract or ability/disability that are relevant to the game. In this way the participants can take an informed decision on whether they wish to proceed.

2. *Dividing the group* – for many games it is necessary to divide people into groups or pairs. Do so *before* embarking on an explanation of what you want the groups or pairs to do. A frequent mistake of trainers is to give their participants too many instructions at once and then wonder why they can't get on with the game. Methods of dividing participants into groups include:

   (i) allowing participants to divide themselves, which ensures they take responsibility for their own operation;

   (ii) asking them to work with "someone you've worked with least", which encourages participants to take that responsibility seriously;

   (iii) allowing participants to work with their neighbour, which risks them working with someone they know already;

   (iv) numbering people into groups ("1, 2, 3, . . ."), which is a good way to separate neighbours;

   (v) placing coloured discs on the seats of participants, which is a good way of manipulatively mixing cliques;

   (vi) putting up a list of syndicate members, useful where you have identified a common feature of some group members that is relevant to the game, such as when you wish to distribute a certain kind of experience (such as management) around the syndicates;

   (vii) separating the group into segments such as front/back or left/right. *Do* remember that your right is the participant's left!

(viii) divide the group by arbitrary categories (like men/ women, those who do/do not wear glasses).

These ways all have their advantages and disadvantages, and you will have to decide which are most appropriate to your group. I find point (iii) above least preferable because it encourages pairs to endure through the whole course.

After that you may have to ask members of groups or pairs to take on different roles (as in **Sabotage** where there are three roles). Asking participants to label themselves as A and B (and C) seems to work well. The group members should choose their labels, and the trainer then explains what the roles mean afterwards.

3. *The introduction* – at this stage you can (usually) give the title of the game and explain the rules. The form of words used in introducing a game can be very important. For example, in the game **Number Crunches** (p. 97) if you do not make it clear that a person who is not part of a cluster cannot be *forced* to leave and can seek to join any group he or she wishes, then nobody will try to do so. One of the important learning points (and a lot of the fun) of the game will be lost. Make sure that participants understand the timings of the game. Use eye contact and humour and, where you can, respond to the apparent reactions of your participants.

4. *The demonstration* – some people follow instructions best by being told, others by reading, and still others by seeing something done. A good trainer will explain the game and then demonstrate it with one or two of the participants. Inexperienced trainers often convince themselves that the group understands a verbal instruction (often after asking an undirected closed leading question like "you all understand, don't you?" and not waiting for an answer), and start the game immediately. They are then surprised that the participants are confused about what they are supposed to do.

5. *The clarification* – ask whether clarification is necessary, and make eye contact with each group member while doing so.

6. *Playing the game* – the most straightforward part of the game. The degree of participation of the trainer and his or her non-verbal communication will be crucial in determining the pace of the game.

7. *Observing the game* – even if the trainer is taking part in the game, he or she will also be observing it with a view to later feedback and to even aborting the game if necessary (either because a game is not going well or because of some unforeseen event – a participant looking very ill or leaving the room without explanation, for instance). If you are in any doubt at all about

21

how a participant is coping with the activity then call a halt and deal with the matter openly.

8. *Stopping playing the game* – knowing when to stop a game is important. Trainers who are not confident about an activity can often abort a game too early. Circle, relay and concentric circle games have a natural end. Others do not. The timer I use has a dial that can be "fiddled" if I want to give the group more or less time than they are "supposed" to have.

9. *Feelings* – people will often want to express how they felt about a game. It is tempting to try and deal with this at the same time as discussing the learning points of the game. I would discourage this. In a game where feelings have been raised then a circular sharing of these can usefully precede a discussion of what the participants learned. If you are going to do "feelings first", though, then do make this clear to the group.

10. *Feedback discussion* – if timing slips then it is tempting for a trainer to skimp on the discussion phase of a game. From the learning point of view, though, the discussion is the most important element of the game, without which it can seem to be a pointless activity. This is the difference between "games" and "playing". It effects the transfer of learning, and ensures that the covert learning objectives of the game for the trainer are achieved. The trainer, however, should accept the learning points made by the group even if they were not the ones that she or he had in mind in using the game. The trainer may want to add other points or seek clarification and to move on to deeper levels of discussion if they are necessary to meet the objectives of the game. For example, whether **Truth Option** (p. 123) is being used as a validation exercise, a self-disclosure exercise or an energizer will crucially affect the level of discussion. If important points take a while to emerge then make a mental note of this and consider varying your introduction of the game. The trainer's listening skills are important in obtaining the most from the participants here, and also in modelling active listening for them. In many games this experience takes place largely in small groups. It is not necessary, helpful or even possible for the trainer to know everything that a participant has gained from a game.

11. *Ending* – it is important to round a game off well. Common criticisms are that participants did not feel that the discussion resolved all possible points, and that they did not understand the reason for the game. It is the responsibility of the trainer to dispose of any "unfinished business" before moving too far away from a game. She or he should also be prepared to state why the activity was suggested in the first place, but it is not unreasonable to offer a detailed explanation (if this is demanded

to a particular individual) *outside* the main sessions of the course. It is also necessary, as Van Ments (1989) has discussed, to deal with any emotions that have been aroused, and to ensure that the issues brought up have been fully dealt with.

Two techniques I use in ending games are *Un-roling* and *Earthing*.

> *Un-roling* – after a role play it is important to ensure that participants are not perceived to be in the role that they took on for the whole of the rest of the course: this can be achieved by un-roling. Members of pairs ask each other "how are you different from . . . ?" and then repeat back the answers. The game **Mind Scan** (p. 90) includes a more elaborate version of this de-briefing.
>
> *Earthing* – after a reflective exercise it is important to restore participants to the "here and now". The game **Here And Now** (p. 78) should be used after any exercise where the trainer thinks this may happen, and at the end of each day before the finishing exercises.

"And now let's do something else" is a poor though not infrequent ending for a game. I like acknowledge the participation of the group and thank them for their contributions to the processing.

It is possible to memorize the most important of these stages by the mnemonic **PERNOD**

Propose the game

Explain what to do

Rehearse the game

eNact the game itself

Observe

Discussion

How to run games together

A course will consist of a series of games linked with many other activities. Without straying into the vast area of course design, I would like to stress the importance of structuring activities properly. The games should have a proper context, and should be led into and go somewhere in terms of the overall aims of the course. Each game must have objectives for the trainer (though of course it could serve additional functions for the other participants). The trainer should ensure that his or her justification for using the game is met during the course. Variety in the type of game used is important. I find that it best to have only one of some types of game on a course (such as auction games). Also, try to ensure that participants never feel herded around, lost or confused.

Games and courses

There are two situations when you will have to co-ordinate the use of games. These are firstly: if you are part of a training community (a group of trainers working together on a batch of courses) and secondly, if you are training the same staff on a series of courses, something that often happens on in-house competency or career milestone-based training, this is particularly useful. Clearly, you can't use the same games on every course or the participants will become bored by them. They may suffer the fate of one of my own participants who not only had to do **RSVP** (p. 109) twice on different courses, but found herself composing the invitation to the five-year-old child both times! Even the **Cocktail Party** introductions exercise (p. 54) can create a very negative first impression if a participant has played it on three successive courses. Such problems may mean that trainers on some courses are forbidden to use certain games: this may seem heavy-handed, but it is necessary in the interests of the participants. Of course, the best way around this is to have as wide as possible a repertoire of games, and to keep adding to it.

The way forward

Finally, I would suggest that the value of games in training depends on the effort that a trainer puts into them outside as well as inside the course-room. There is no such thing as an off-the-peg training activity any more than there is an off-the-peg training course (though many training consultants and publishers will try to convince you otherwise!). Perhaps we should be thankful for this, because if there were then there would be off-the-peg trainers too! The value of the activities in this book depends on the effort that you put into asking questions like:

How could this activity be improved?
How could this activity be made more relevant to my delegates?
What variations could I make to this activity?
Are there any other training objectives which this activity could meet?

I would very much welcome feedback from readers on any of these questions.

2

The objectives used in this book

The activities in this book are indexed by the nature of their learning objective (see pp. 157–61). The specific objectives of each session will have to be formulated by the trainer, if appropriate, in the usual "by the end of the session participants will be able to . . ." formula. I have used the following definitions:

- *Action planning* – an essential part of any course will be the element of action planning in which participants seek to apply what they have learned to their work.
- *Assertiveness* – the distinction between assertive, aggressive and passive behaviour patterns is frequently made in social and life skills training. For a history of the concept of assertiveness see Rakos (1986).
- *Attention switching* – activities with a high reflective content can leave delegates thinking too hard and long about the issues raised for them when there are other matters to be covered on the course. One way of overcoming this is through a quick attention switching exercise. Most of them are also energizers, but are here being used for a slightly different purpose.
- *Attributions* – courses on equal opportunities frequently explore the question of attributions – the assumptions that can be made about people belonging to a particular group of category. In this connection I also include attributions made of other course members or about other people in a working group – which may be explored in a team-building course.
- *Creativity* – this refers to the development of the ability to find new ideas and concepts rather than the solving of practical problems, though the same exercises may often be used for both purposes.
- *Decision making* – most of these activities concern the process of decision making in groups.

- *Energizer* – at certain times on a course (the "pudding session" first thing after lunch is a classic instance), participants will lack energy and concentration. An energizer is an activity with no other purpose than to get the blood flowing and to re-establish a group after a break, usually through physical activity. They should be used enthusiastically but carefully, since delegates with a cynical approach to participative training tend to react particularly negatively to these apparently purposeless activities. I keep a few energizers in reserve, and allow any member of the group to ask for an energizer. If the feeling of the group is that one is needed then it can be brought in. I would not recommend using the same energizer twice on a course.
- *Expectations* – it is often useful in a course to establish the expectations that group members have brought with them.
- *Feedback* – the principles of feedback may well be covered before a game begins if participants have to give feedback to one another. They can usually form part of a group contract (see pp. 16–18). Feedback will often be an objective in its own right (for example, in appraisal interviewing training), and the principles set out on p. 10 can form the basis of the input part of such a session.
- *Introductions* – a repertoire of introduction exercises is useful. If you are part of a training community it is a good idea to allocate these to specific courses. Energizers can help to break the tension during the introductory phase of the group life. Used at this point, they are often referred to as "icebreakers."
- *Listening skills* – a wide variety of active listening skills and non-verbal sensitivities can be taught through the use of games. They are of use in a whole range of courses covering personal effectiveness, workplace skills, counselling and customer care.
- *Motivation* – the objective of asking participants to question their own motivation can be important in allowing them to consider alternative courses of action (for example, on culture change programmes). It can also form part of management training where delegates are trying to improve their own understanding of the principles of human motivation.
- *Negotiation* – where groups have shared resources then negotiation must take place to ensure that the needs of all those involved are met. Most leadership courses will require this objective to be included.
- *Non-verbal communication* – most of the games in this book can be used to heighten sensitivity to non-verbal signals. With the games indicated this is particularly the case, and they might be useful on courses with customer care or face-to-face communication themes.
- *Problem solving* – the distinction between problem solving and

creativity has been described above. The emphasis here is on the solving of practical problems using all of the resources available in an effective and efficient manner.

- *Sabotage* – there may be a tendency for some participants to seek to sabotage aspects of a training course. It is therefore a good idea for trainers to have exercises that allow this tendency to be dealt with openly. Sabotage is something that delegates may well have to deal with themselves, and so it has even more reason to be a legitimate training objective.
- *Self-disclosure* – this can sometimes be useful in its own right to establish a culture of frankness and trust, but it is also an important part of self-development and team-building courses. During self-disclosure games it is often useful to remind the group of the confidentiality terms of their contract.
- *Self-perception* – an increase in understanding of how one is, and the relationship between that and the way that one is perceived by other people.
- *Team-building* – many objectives centre on encouraging teams to be more effective at working together. Most of the games in this book can be steered in this direction through correct processing, but for some it is important enough to have a specific objective.
- *Trainer training* – it is possible to use any of the games in this book for trainer training, but there are some which are especially well suited to this purpose and they have been indicated by reference to this objective.
- *Trust* – to impart an understanding of the preconditions necessary to trust someone, and the degree to which that trust is extended.
- *Validation* – these exercises will assess the learning of some particular skill or knowledge covered elsewhere on a course, or help ascertain the impressions of a group of participants of a course or any of its activities. (This must be differentiated from the *evaluation* of the worth of the objectives of the course to the client.)
- *Verbal/written communication* – these core areas of training need no explanation.

3

The games

Activity Mime
Amnesia
Am/Seem
Appreciative Disagreements
Are You Sitting Comfortably?
Badgering
Bit Parts Of Speech
Body Hello
Chain Mime
The Chairs
Challenge Challenge
Charoodles
Circular Reactions
Cocktail Party
Consensus
Convoy
Cursed Assumptions
Elementary
Exotic Fruits
Family Reunion
Fangs
Fantasies
First Impressions
Fists
Fruit Relay
Good Grief
Great Expectations
Group Sculpture
Hand To Mouth
Here And Now
Interviews
Invisible Tug-Of-War

Just A Minute
Knotty Problems
Labels
Lies! Lies
Listening Limbs
Martians
Mind Scan
Mirrors
Mornington Crescent
Mutual Introductions
Name Plate Shuffle
Number Crunches
One Pound Auction
On Your Face
Pickpockets
Possibilities
Problems Without Words
Re-Inventing The Wheel
RSVP
Rude Aerobics
Rules Of The Game
Sabotage
Selves And Possibilities
Silent Meal/Silent Walk
Statue Stop
Stamps
Time Lapse
Time Lines
Tones Of Voice
Truth Option
Ugly Sisters

Voluntaries

War Of Words

Waxworks

What'll Be My Line?

Wheel Of Experience

Whirlpool

Whispers

Who's Who?

Wibble-Wobble

Will To Live

Word Search

You Spy

Activity Mime

Summary   Participants guess hobbies and interests mimed by each other.

Objective   Introductions.

Materials   None.

Timing   15 minutes.

Procedure
1. Form the group into a circle where the participants can all see each other.
2. Ask them to think of an interest of theirs that they can act out.
3. Each person does their mime (including the group leader).
4. Explain that the game will progress by participants recalling each other's mimes. They will clap their hands, do their own mime, clap their hands again, point to someone else and do the other person's mime. Demonstrate this once for you copying another person, and once for another person copying your mime. The person pointed to repeat this, silently correcting any mime that was not accurate.

Variations
1. This can be developed into a knockout after a few rounds until only one person is left.
2. Ask participants to copy two mimes, followed by two responses.
3. The mime can be to do with the kind of work they do, how they are feeling at the moment, or any other attribute.

Amnesia

Summary   Identifying a label that cannot be seen.

Objectives   Verbal communication.
Feedback.

Materials   Sticky labels.
Pens.

Timing   15 minutes.

Procedure
1. Hand out the sticky labels, blank and with the backing on them. Ask participants to put the name of a well known dead person on them.
2. Ask them to put their label on the forehead of another person *without them seeing what the label says*.
3. Explain that they are suffering from amnesia and cannot remember who they are. Invite them to mill around to find out who they are *using only questions that can be answered "yes" or "no"*.
4. Discuss how difficult the exercise was and how limiting the questions were.

Commentary This is a variation on **Labels** (p. 83).

Variations
1. When participants mill around suggest they react as they would to the real person (exaggerating if they wish).
2. Use living people, fictional characters, TV personalities or any other category that the group comes up with.
3. Use prepared labels.
4. Shuffle the labels and put them on heads yourself.
5. Use labels showing moods and feelings.
6. Allow participants to use open questions.

34

Am/Seem

Summary   Exploration of how group members see themselves and are seen by others.

Objectives   Self-disclosure.
Team-building.
Assertiveness.

Materials   Prepared cards (see below).
One card for each group member with his or her name on it.
Pens.
Pins.

Timing   30 minutes.

Procedure
1. Pin up the name cards round the room at an equal distance from each other.
2. Give each participant a set of the prepared cards and explain that each person has the same ones. You may wish to eliminate some items or add others, depending on the level of trust established within the group.
3. Invite participants to pin the cards under the name of the person they consider most appropriate. If you think it will help the group then start them with their own name and ask them to move clockwise at the same time so that nobody knows who has given what card to whom.
4. Invite them to circulate and look at their own and others' lists.
5. Discuss the extent to which people's perceptions of themselves differed from those of others. Note how this can even apply to apparently "objective" categories like height.

Commentary On a team-building course it will not be appropriate to include the trainer. In other contexts it might.

Variations
1. Give different people different but overlapping sets of cards.
2. Provide some blank cards for people to put their own categories.

3. In the discussion, ask what other categories people would have liked to have.
4. Use blank cards only.

Sample cards

Person who makes me laugh the most.
Kindest person.
Most outgoing person.
Most hard working person.
Most perceptive person.
Untidiest person.
Most reliable person.
Friendliest person.
Silliest person.
Most unreliable person.
Most scatterbrained person.
Most flexible person.
Most trustworthy person.
Most serious person.
Most prejudiced person.
Most critical person.
Person I would most share my feelings with.
Most talkative person.
Most spiritual person.
Most untrustworthy person.
Most artistic person.
Person who most often irritates me.
Youngest person.
Cleverest person.
Most logical person.
Most accepting person.
Least prejudiced person.
Wisest person.
Most passive person.
Person I would most like to work with.
Most cynical person.
Oldest person.
Greediest person.
Person I would most like to go on holiday with.
Most generous person.
Smartest person.
Person who made the least impression on me.
Most fashionable person.
Person I would most like to be my boss.
Most beautiful person.
Most aggressive person.

Sexiest person.
Person who is most often right.
Calmest person.
Most confident person.
Person who is most often wrong.
Most lively person.
Most uncritical person.
Most unpredictable person.
Most approachable person.
Saddest person.
Tallest person.
Shortest person.
Bravest person.

Appreciative Disagreements

Summary   Participants try to change each other's minds while the other person practises non-confrontational responses.

Objectives   Non-verbal communication.
Motivation.
Assertiveness.

Materials   None.

Timing   20 minutes.

Procedure   1.   Ask participants to work in pairs and choose a topic on which they will disagree. It does not matter if they both have the same view.
2.   Invite them to take opposing views and do all they can to persuade the other to change his/her mind. Explain that at a signal they will swap over roles. Responses should be in the form *"I appreciate/I agree/I respect . . . AND"* (note "and" and not "but").
3.   On a signal ask them to exchange roles.

Commentary   Often those who have started arguing against their "natural" view report difficulty in changing back to what they "really" believe. Explore how the acknowledgement in the form of words used affected their ability to take a hostile attitude. This is a good exercise to do immediately after **War of Words**. You may wish to have said something about the theory of assertiveness before starting on this exercise.

Are you Sitting Comfortably

Summary Story-telling exercise.

Objectives Listening skills.

Materials Whiteboard and pens.

Timing 30 minutes.

Procedure

1. This session works best after an explanation of the nature of paraphrasing (of facts and of feelings) and types of question (for example, open, closed, rhetorical, multiple, leading) which can be covered in the processing of **Sabotage** (p. 112). Start by saying "Please put your pens and paper away. I am going to tell you a story." Wait until they have done so and then begin to tell your story.

2. The story should be based on your own experience (with an element of self-disclosure) and have a fair number of details such as names and dates. It should take no more than five minutes to tell. An example of one of my stories is given below.

3. Say "I would like you to tell me as much as you can remember about the story." Put up the points on the whiteboard, allowing space between lines. If there is disagreement then put up all versions unless the group comes to agree on one version. Do not correct mistakes. Make the point that the group have between them remembered more than any one individual but that even on factual matters there can be differences of opinion about material recalled from only a few minutes previously.

4. Find out why the group did not ask questions. Bring out the learning point about the nature of interruptions and when interventions are (i) expected and (ii) useful. Then ask what questions people would *like* to have asked and put them up in a different colour.

5. Answer the questions if you wish.

Commentary It is advisable to have at least three stories to tell in this game, as

39

the constant repetition of one story tends to make it seem rather scripted. You may well find that delegates will ask some quite probing questions about your story, so it is a good idea to think in advance what your level of self-disclosure will be.

Sample story It was a warm afternoon in April 1987. John, Paul, Lucy and I had decided to go out to the cinema. We met at King's Cross and went to a pub called the Clarence for a drink. I had a gin and tonic, John had a lager, Paul had a Guinness and Lucy had an orange juice. After that we went to the Scala Cinema, on the corner of Pentonville Road, where we saw a double bill. I like the Scala because they do home made cakes there and they have a lovely little tabby cat named Fritz. I remember that one of the movies was *Fantasia* but I can't remember the name of the other one. I enjoyed the films very much. At eight thirty we left the Scala and were thinking about where to eat when we came to King's Cross station. We could see flashing blue lights from the front of the station, a crowd of people and then, as we got closer, the fire engines. I was frightened, this was the first time that I had ever seen a dead body. We stayed for about twenty minutes and then realized that we would have to find an alternative way home. John and Paul got a taxi to South Kensington. Lucy and I started to walk down to Russell Square station. In the square people were going about their business, talking and drinking and I felt very upset and wanted to go up to someone and say "how can you act like this when there are people being burned alive up the road?" I had to walk all the way to Embankment station and did not get home until very late that evening. It was not until I listened to the news the next morning that I realized the extent of the tragedy that I had almost become a part of.

Badgering

Summary   Participants pass information on about each other with their badges.

Objectives   Introductions.
Listening skills.

Materials   Name badges.

Timing   20 minutes at least.

Procedure   1.   Ask participants to work in pairs. They are to spend five minutes at the end of which each will have introduced him or herself. Then ask them to exchange name badges.
2.   Ask participants to find a new partner and (from a distance) to show the badge, point to who it belongs to, and say as much as they can remember about that person.
3.   Reverse roles and then exchange badges.
4.   Ask participants to find another new partner and (from a distance) to show the badge, point to who it belongs to, and say as much as they can remember about that person. Reverse roles and exchange badges again.
5.   Repeat until the only person to whom the badge has not been introduced is the original partner. This *should* happen at the same time for everybody, but it probably won't. Then ask participants to introduce that person to the others. Explain that some of the information will have become distorted and that they should not worry about getting anything wrong. Participants can correct any information about themselves that has become distorted.
6.   Hold a discussion on why information became changed.

Commentary If there is an odd number of participants, the trainer will have to take part to even the numbers.

Variations   1.   A simpler session has participants keeping the first badge they exchanged and introducing that person to each of the others. The discussion will centre on how the information they conveyed about that person changed.

2. Some training organizations use cardboard triangular "toblerones" to mark places and these can be used instead of badges.

3. Where participants all have them they can use their business cards.

Bit Parts of Speech

Summary   Personifying different parts of speech, course members construct sentences.

Objective   Written communication (to establish how types of words are used to construct sentences).

Materials   Whiteboard.
Coloured whiteboard markers.
Prepared cards with the names of the parts of speech and an example (conjunction, interjection, preposition, verb, adverb, noun, article, adjective and pronoun).

Timing   15 minutes.

Procedure   1. Allocate to each participant the name of a part of speech and ensure that they know what that part of speech means, giving examples where necessary.
2. Ask participants to construct a sentence one word at a time on the whiteboard using pens of different colours. They score if their word could be grammatically correct in the sentence as written so far. The others can challenge. If challenged and they can complete the sentence grammatically, they score three points for an incorrect challenge. If not then the challenger gains two points.

Commentary If a participant objects that some parts of speech naturally score more than others, being more frequently used in English, then make this into a learning point. It is advisable to have a reference source for participants (like Bryson 1990), and a dictionary for arbitration.

Body Hello

Summary   Subjects say "hello" with different parts of their bodies.

Objectives   Introductions.
Energizer.

Materials   Lively music (like Vivaldi's *Four Seasons*).

Timing   Ten minutes.

Procedure

1.   Have the music playing from the start of the exercise, preferably when the participants are entering the room.
2.   Stand in the middle of the room. Over the music explain that introductions are often difficult and that you would like members to try introducing themselves to each other one part of the body at a time. Continue "First I'm going to ask you to introduce yourself to someone with your elbow."
3.   Go through different parts of the body such as foot, knee, buttocks, shoulder and finally voice.
4.   In discussion consider the difference that the non-verbal aspect of the introduction made to the process of getting acquainted.

Commentary   This exercise should be energetically modelled by the trainer. It is best done as the first thing on a course. I have found it particularly effective on counselling courses where the non-verbal aspects of interactions have to be examined in some detail.

Chain Mime

Summary   Imitation exercise based on mime.

Objective   Non-verbal communication.

Materials   None.

Timing   Five minutes for each pair in the group.

Procedure
1. Ask for two volunteers, and ask all other group members to leave the room.
2. Explain to the pair left that the objective of the game is to carry out a mime which will be observed and copied by another pair. Ask them to choose a subject. If they are unable to think of one then take one from the list below.
3. After they have practiced a couple of times, ask a second pair into the room and have them observe the mime. Make it clear that there is to be no talking between the pairs.
4. The first pair then go to the side of the room while the second pair demonstrate the mime to a third pair and so on, until the last pair is reached. This pair then has to guess what the mime represents.
5. Discuss how the mime has changed and why.

Commentary   The mime should be done efficiently and in detail but fairly briskly or the momentum of the game will be lost. If there is an odd number of people in the group then the singleton can be the guesser at the end.

Variation   Allow the other people into the room to copy the mime individually and then send them out again without assembling the whole group until the very end of the game.

Possible mimes

The wedding photographs.
Making meringues.

45

Mending a puncture.
Weeding the garden.
Walking the dog.
Wheel-clamping a car.
Dictating a letter.
Changing the duvet cover.
Exchanging birthday presents.
Lighting a pipe.
Cashing a postal order.
Polishing shoes.
Cleaning a bike.

The Chairs

Summary   In pairs participants try and persuade each other to get up off a chair.

Materials   A hard chair.

Timing   30 minutes.

Objectives   Assertiveness.
Non-verbal communication.

Procedure
1. Ask for a volunteer and sit them in the chair in the centre. Ask for another volunteer.
2. Explain that the task of the second volunteer is to persuade the first to get out of the chair. If they wish they can dramatize a situation which they might be in and take that as their starting point (examples below). They may not touch the person, but may say anything they like, and it is up to the person sitting whether she or he vacates the seat.
3. Invite another pair to try.
4. Lead a discussion. Discover the kinds of arguments people used. Why did they think that argument would work? Were they the ones that they would have liked used on them? Would you let anything work on you? If not, why not? Often a simple "I would feel better if you stood up" works. If they have a dramatized situation then explore other options. Consider whose rights (if anyone's) were in danger of being violated. Consider the non-verbal communication used by the parties.

Commentary This is based on the same game type as **Fists** (p. 68).

Variations
1. Instead of asking for a second volunteer invite the rest of the group to take turns in improvising. This "brainstorm" approach can work well.
2. The first three stages can be done by the whole group in pairs.

Situation examples

> Finding someone in your seat at the theatre.
> Returning to find your seat occupied on a train.
> Finding "your" seat taken in the course-room on the second day.
> Being a clumsy waiter.
> Head waiter trying to close a restaurant.
> Operating an electric chair.
> Being an office cleaner.
> Sitting in an aircraft that is about to crash.
> Mother telling her child to come in for dinner.
> Deck-chair attendant.
> Dentist.
> Officer evacuating the *Titanic*.
> Nurse getting a patient back into bed.
> Elderly person needing a seat on the underground.

Challenge Challenge

Summary   Developing responses to challenges.

Objectives   Assertiveness.
Equal opportunities.
Trainer training (or any other area where challenging skills are being developed).

Materials   Plain paper in as many colours as you have groups.
Discs (1″ in diameter) of the same colours as the paper.
Pens.
Chairs.

Timing   One hour.

Procedure
1. Form an even number of groups according to the colour of the discs on people's chairs and give each group the paper of the same colour. Groups should ideally be of three to five members.
2. Ask group members to write a statement on the card that provokes the kind of challenge that the session is about (for example, racist remarks, training confrontations). These are to be placed face down in the centre of the room.
3. Invite groups to pick up one challenge for each member of the group. They should not choose "their" colour.
4. Ask participants to prepare, in groups according to their discs, answers to those challenges. In doing so they should think about:

   (i) Ways to close the topic;
   (ii) Ways to ensure the other person understands why what they say is being challenged;
   (iii) Anticipating any comments that might follow-on from the original comment and deal with them.

5. Groups then pair up. One group will give its challenges to the other group, who will deliver them back. The first group will respond according to the strategy they have prepared. They

49

will have a spokesperson who responds with the others "behind the curtain" offering suggestions.

6. Ensure that the group issuing the challenge gives feedback on what were the most and least effective challenges and why this was the case. Then repeat Stages 5 and 6 with reversed roles.

Commentary A commonly ineffective challenge is "You must see that . . ." Confrontational responses tend to provoke further disagreement.

Variation Where there are about a dozen people in the group then Stages 5 and 6 can be carried out in plenary.

Charoodles

Summary   A relay activity in which participants take it in turn to solve and draw anagrams for the other team members to guess.

Materials   Prepared anagrams.
Pens.
Paper.
Clipboards.
Chairs.

Timing   15 minutes.

Objectives Non-verbal communication.
Attention switching.
Energizer.
Creativity.

Procedure   1. Ask the group to form teams and to arrange their team in chairs in a "bus" formation so one is sitting at the front and the others fanned out behind.
2. Give pens and paper to the person in front. Explain the rules, which are that:
(a) the person in front comes to the trainer to pick up an anagram;
(b) s/he solves it then draws it. The others have to guess what it is but the trainer can only nod or shake his or her head;
(c) another member of the group takes the front seat and this continues until all have had a turn;
(d) the first team to finish wins.
3. You may hint at a theme for the anagrams suitable for the group (like computing words, training words).

Commentary The anagrams should be simple. If the game is run briskly then participants will not worry about their drawing ability. The title is a combination of "charades" and "doodles".

Variation   Stage (b) can be to act out the anagram rather than draw it. This will make the game take rather longer.

Circular Reactions

Summary   Energizer in which participants reform circle with their eyes closed.

Objectives   Energizer.
Attention switching.

Materials   None.

Timing   10 minutes.

Procedure
1. Ask participants to choose an identifying noise and to make it to the rest of the group. It should be different to everyone else's.
2. Ensure that everyone is clear as to the noises of their partners left and right.
3. Ask them to move to different parts of the room and to reform the circle with their eyes closed by identifying the right noises and moving towards them.

Cocktail Party

Summary   Introductions exercise simulating cocktail party conversations.

Objective   Introductions.

Materials   Whiteboard and pens (optional).

Timing   30 minutes (ten minutes to mingle and five minutes per person). With a large group this can become a very time-consuming activity.

Procedure
1. Participants are asked to imagine that they are at a cocktail party. They are each to find out (for later sharing with the rest of the group) three different things about three different people. Participants must not disclose the same information to a different questioner.
2. After five minutes, form the group into a circle and process the findings. Invite people to add to what has been said about them.

Commentary You may wish to give guidance about the sorts of information exchanged; for example, about work, feelings, the course, personal background.

Variations
1. The trainer can put up a grid on the whiteboard of group members' names on which they can put up facts as they find them out. This forms the starting point for the discussion phase.
2. If you ask participants to enter fully into the spirit of the cocktail party you can then process the feelings: for example, did they take the initiative or wait for someone to talk to them – in what other situations do they feel like that? If this is the objective then it is possible to dispense with the exchange of information.
3. Encourage participants in their pairs to disclose the results of a previous exercise.

54

Consensus

Summary   A group decision-making activity.

Objectives Team-building.
Assertiveness.
Decision making.

Materials   Checklists (see below).
Pens.

Timing   One hour.

Procedure
1. Hand out the checklist and ask participants to rank their ten most important qualities in descending order of importance. When they have done so, ask them to remove the five lowest.
2. Ask the group to come to a consensus as to which are the most important qualities in a 20 minute period. Observe them doing so.
3. Discuss with the group how they came to the consensus they reached.

Commentary The group may well seek further advice on terms of reference, or complain that the task is too hard. The trainer should remain outside the group and not offer directive advice. If the group abandons a constraint like **Pillow Talk** then this should be allowed and then talked through in the discussion phase.

Variations
1. If your learning points are about team-building then at Stage 2 ask group members to rank each member according to how dominant they think they are. Share these and get each person to work out their average rank (the total score they have been given by themselves and others divided by number of people in the group). A *low* score means they are perceived as *dominant*. Divide the group into sub-groups according to dominance and then go through Stage 2.
2. It is possible to use other qualities like "Qualities of an effective

manager" elicited through brainstorming the whole group, if that is something that can be drawn on later in the course.

3. The group processes can be recorded by the trainer using video and/or an interaction analysis like that of Bales (Swenson 1973, pp. 195–207) or Rackham (1977). This will increase the processing time considerably.

Personal qualities checklist

To me it is important that another person can:

- have a good sense of humour
- be kind
- have fun
- be understanding
- be friendly
- be outrageous
- be trustworthy
- be outgoing
- take a joke
- be honest
- be critical
- be able to understand my feelings
- be talkative
- be able to listen
- be creative
- be stylish
- be spontaneous
- be mature
- be child-like
- be wise
- state their bottom line
- be logical
- be accepting
- know a lot
- listen
- be cynical
- be generous
- be confident
- be consistent
- be attractive
- be calm
- understand me
- be correct
- be aggressive
- be in control
- be doing the best you can
- be lively
- be predictable

Convoy

Summary   One group tries to cross the room and another has to stop them.

Objectives   Energizer.
Attention switching.

Materials   None.

Timing   Five minutes.

Procedure
1. Invite participants to form two teams. One team is the convoy and the other the interceptors.
2. Instruct the convoy to get from one end of the room to the other, and the other group has to stop them from doing so.
3. Explain that both groups must retain linked hands throughout.

Commentary   This can be a very energetic energizer and is therefore one where the precaution of asking participants to take their shoes off first could be used.

Variation   Each group can be asked to act as interceptors for the other group.

Cursed Assumptions

Summary Exploration of prejudice and reactions to it.

Objectives Attributions.

Materials Prepared cards (one for each person).
Blank cards (one per participant).
Pens.

Timing At least one hour.

Procedure
1. Read out the prepared cards and put them face down in a pile. Ask participants to write one *other* basis of prejudice on their card and put them on the pile.
2. Shuffle the cards and invite group members to take one card each.
3. Form pairs and ask group members to take it in turns to announce the subject on their card, after which their partner is to make as many stereotyped remarks as they can. Then the person with the card defends that group against the comments. Then exchange roles.
4. Reform the group and discuss the statements made, how generally they were believed to be valid, the feelings people had when giving or receiving the remarks and what that tells group members about their own stereotypes.

Commentary There is an element of risk in allowing participants to insult each other on the basis of qualities that may actually apply to them. It is therefore vital that this exercise be fully processed and that all feelings raised are fully discussed. It is, however, a very powerful way of examining the feeling of being a victim of prejudice.

Variations
1. The categories can be generated from the group itself before the game commences.
2. Participants can be given one opportunity to exchange their card if it is a category that they feel uncomfortable with.

Categories of prejudice

Old people	Scots
Catholics	Smokers
Gay men	Police
Jews	Punks
Women	Arabs
Gypsies	Irish
Blacks	Country people
Lesbians	Double glazing sellers
Cyclists	Old people
Tourists	Bus conductors
Plumbers	Trainers
Conservatives	Communists
Foreigners	Children

Elementary

Summary   Deducing things about people from objects they have or use.

Objective   Introductions.

Materials   Pens and paper.

Timing   Ten minutes in pairs and five minutes per person.

Procedure
1. Divide the group into pairs who don't know each other and ask them to label themselves A and B. Explain that A will be the suspect and B the detective.
2. Ask each suspect to draw six items that they have used in the past month. They should choose items which other people can use to guess things about them. It doesn't matter if the drawing is not accurate: it enriches the game.
3. After the deductions have been made reverse the roles. While the detective is making his or her deductions the suspect should not say anything.
4. Bring the group together and have detectives introducing suspects.

Variations
1. The suspect can be allowed to make non-verbal responses.
2. The game can be carried out in the whole group rather than in pairs.
3. The suspect can produce items from his or her pockets or handbag, and the detective can work on those and on cues like dress.

Exotic Fruits

Summary   A centre/circle game in which people are named after exotic fruits.

Objectives   Energizer.
Attention switching.

Materials   Chairs.

Timing   Five minutes, or as long as you wish.

Procedure
1. Form participants in their chairs in a *tight* circle with the trainer in the middle. Go round the circle getting each to name him or her self after an exotic fruit and say the name aloud. Name yourself.
2. Ask for a volunteer and change places with them. Explain that the volunteer is now "It". The objective of "It" is to get out of the centre by putting someone else in. When you (as the last "It") name a fruit aloud then "It" has to touch everyone's knees in succession starting with yours with the objective of reaching the person named *before* they can call out the name of another fruit.
3. If the named fruit fails to name another in time then he or she becomes "It". If he or she succeeds then "It" tries to reach that person before they name a third fruit, and so on.
4. If anyone calls out their own fruit, the fruit of the person who is "It" or a fruit that is not in the game at all then they become "It".
5. Have a trial run and then ask participants to call out their fruits again so everyone can remind themselves.
6. Proceed with the game.

Commentary This is a difficult game to explain before you start, so do a few trial rounds first. But it is a lively energizer, and is good for the end of a day. It usually ends up with the whole group in hysterics. If the trainer does a practice run with a fruit name that has not been used, then that name will often turn up later in the game.

List of fruits Apricot, avocado, banana, breadfruit, cacao, cantaloupe, citrus, clementine, date, fig, grape, kiwifruit, kumquat, lemon, lime, lychee, melon, nectarine, olive, orange, pawpaw, papaya, passionfruit, persimmon, pineapple, pomegranate, tamarind, tangerine, ugli fruit.

Variation After a specified number of turns as "It" participants go out, the circle closes up and others become "It" for mentioning their fruit.

Family Reunion

Summary   Making card to send to a person of unspecified gender.

Objective   Attributions.

Materials   A wide variety of magazines.
Paper.
Scissors.
Glue.
Pens.
Cartridge paper.

Timing   One hour.

Procedure   1. Explain that participants have been contacted from Lima, Peru
with a message stating that a long-lost cousin has been discovered. The message is rather garbled and all you know is
that the name is "Terri" and that they are going to get married
next week.
2. Their task is to individually design a wedding card, completed
and signed. Introduce the material and ask what assumptions
they will have to make about Terri. If the point is not made by
them, note that they have not yet established whether Terri is
a man or a woman.
3. Share the results with the rest of the group and consider how
attributions colour our judgement.

Variations   1. Change the situation to a birthday, a bereavement, christening
of a child of unspecified gender, etc.
2. Send participants out to a shop to look at the real cards, make
comparisons and write letters to the card manufacturers.

Fangs

Summary   Tag game in which participants avoid becoming vampires.

Objectives   Energizer.
Attention switching.
Trust exercise.

Materials   Blindfolds.

Timing   Ten minutes.

Procedure
1. Explain that all participants will be blindfolded and one or two (depending on the size of the group) are touched on the shoulder, at which point they become vampires.
2. They can create further vampires by grabbing people's throats and growling very loudly.
3. The game ends when everyone has been turned into a vampire.

Commentary The trainers do not wear blindfolds.

Fantasies

Summary   Development and sharing of fantasies.

Objective   Self-disclosure.

Materials   None.

Timing   30 minutes.

Procedure

1. Start the game when the group are informally distributed. Ask participants to imagine that they can be anything they want to and to write down *three* fantasies that they have as to what they would like to be or to do (not to have) if there were no limits on them. Emphasize that during this exercise they will not be asked to disclose anything to other group members that they do not want to.

2. Ask participants to delete the *two* which are least important and to write down five *reasons* why that remaining fantasy is important to them. Ask them to choose the three reasons that are the most important.

3. Form the participants into twos and threes (as numbers fit) to discuss what the process has resulted in. Allow ten minutes for this.

4. In a general discussion, consider what the results suggest about the needs we have, and the alternative ways in which they may be satisfied.

5. Allow a short period of action planning in which participants think about alternative ways in which they might realize the needs that they have identified.

Commentary In the discussion you may wish to refer to some of the theories of needs such as those of Maslow or Herzberg. Ribeaux and Poppleton (1978) offer a good introduction.

First Impressions

Summary   Exercise exchanging first impressions.

Objectives   Self-perception.
                   Self-disclosure.
                   Attribution.

Materials   Paper and pens (optional).
                   Flipchart.

Timing   30 minutes.

Procedure   1. Remind group members of the first time that they saw each
                       other. Introduce an exercise to share these impressions and to
                       consider their accuracy.
                   2. Go through a list of questions on a flipchart:

                       What was your first impression of me?
                       What things about me gave you that impression?
                       Did I remind you of anyone else? Was that important?
                       Do you want to know if that was the impression I wanted to
                       give?
                       How accurate do you now feel the impression you had of me
                       is?

                   3. Invite group members to form pairs and share their first
                       impressions. Say that you will ask them to change after seven
                       minutes.
                   4. After three combinations bring the group back together and ask
                       what people have learned about the first impressions that
                       people make.

Commentary Once participants have started this, they will often want to do it
with everyone else. Time rarely allows this (it can be calculated from
the formula on p. 13). Invite them to continue outside the course
room if necessary. This exercise works best with people who are all
strangers at the start of the course.

Variations 1. Dispense with Stage 4.
2. Have Stage 4 with small groups progressively merging.

Fists

Summary   In pairs, participants try and persuade each other to open their fists.

Objectives Assertiveness.
Non-verbal communication.

Materials   None.

Timing   Ten minutes.

Procedure
1. Ask the group to form pairs, stand up, and one person in each pair to close his/her fist.
2. Explain that the partners have to persuade them to open their fists. They may not touch the person, but may say anything they like, and it is up to the people with their fists closed when they open them.
3. Reverse the roles.
4. Lead a discussion. Discover the kinds of arguments people used. Why did they think that argument would work? Were they the ones that they would have liked used on them? Would they let anything at all work on them? If not, why not? Often a simple "I would feel better if you opened your hand" works.

Commentary This is based on the same game-type as **The Chairs** (p. 47). A related anecdote is that of the ancient monkey trap which worked by placing a fruit in a secure metal vase. Having grasped the fruit the monkey will not let go and is caught.

Variations
1. The activity to be altered can be raising the hand as if to strike, baring teeth, frowning, laughing, bowing, kneeling, smiling, being coiled up, holding feet, etc. If different postures are allocated to different people then the way in which hostile and non-hostile gestures evoke a response in the other and feelings in the self can be explored.
3. Pairs can either be the subjects or objects of persuasion, or both.

3. One or both of the pairs can be standing, sitting, lying down, etc. Variations on this through the group will show some interesting points about posture, relative position and dominance.

Fruit Relay

Summary   Relay game reading passage out loud.

Objectives   Energizer.
Attention switching.

Timing   Ten minutes.

Materials   Prepared lists for words.

Procedure

1. Form participants into two teams and arrange them facing opposite sides of the room. Give the first person in each team a folded piece of paper with a list of about 20 words on it. An example is given below.
2. Explain that this is a relay race and the first team to complete wins. The members of each team will take it in turn to run to the far end of the room, open the piece of paper, read the first words and then fold the paper, run back and pass it to the second person who does the same with the second word, and so forth. When the team members have all run then they do so again in the same order. There are 20 words altogether.
3. Answer any questions and then run the relay.

Commentary   Although this is an energizer, it is possible to take the game further by discussing competitiveness and other feelings of the group.

Variations

1. Use different lists for each group.
2. Have group members run as in a three-legged race.

List of words

Lemon.	Pomegranate.	Carburettor.	Lemon.
Pawpaw.	Lemon.	Melon.	Passionfruit.
Orange.	Lychee.	Pineapple.	Avocado.
Tangerine.	Banana.	Tamarind.	Orange.
Lime.	Olive.	Apricot.	Nectarine.

Good Grief

Summary   Game simulating grief for controlled and uncontrolled loss.

Objectives   Self-perception (through exploring feelings of controlled and uncontrolled loss, used for example in the development of counselling skills).

Materials   Eight blank cards for each person.
Paper.
Pens.

Timing   30 minutes.

Procedure

Part I – Loss

1. Divide the group into fours. Distribute cards to each person.
2. Ask participants to fill the cards with two people who are most important to them, two physical possessions which are most important to them, two activities which are most important to them and two roles in their life which are most important to them.
3. Then explain that they will have to give up *one* of their cards, but that they can choose which one. Collect them in a basket or container. Repeat this twice. Then explain that you are going to take two items, and that this time they have no choice as to which they lose. They must hold out them all (face down). Collect them in.
4. Explore in fours and the group feelings that this evokes.

Part II – Recovery

5. Explain that everyone is going to have restored to them what they have lost. Hand out papers and invite participants to draw a flower with eight petals to represent the eight possible losses, and – if they want – to put the names in them.

Commentary This can be a very powerful exercise and requires a high degree of trust. Group members may have to support each other through the exercise.

Variation The loss can be personified as caused by cancer, HIV or whatever causal agent is most appropriate.

Great Expectations

Summary   An exercise to ascertain the expectations of group members.

Objectives   Expectations.
Objective setting.

Materials   Pens and newsprint.

Timing   Ten minutes plus five minutes for each group of three to four within the course.

Procedure
1. Set whatever limits you have to on what can be contained within the training event. Explain the importance of establishing the expectations of participants before embarking on a training event.
2. Put up on a whiteboard a set of questions taken from the list given below. You may wish to arrange the questions in one of the formats shown on p. 75 which is appropriate to the number of questions asked (this can stimulate creativity more than a piece of newsprint divided into quarters). Emphasize that answers should do justice to each course member, and the group should elect someone to explain their result to the others.
3. Ask participants to form groups of four or five and hand out newsprint. Ask each group to work independently and to elect a speaker to take the other groups through what they produce. Allow about ten minutes for the exercise and then reform the main group.
4. Put newsprint on the walls and explain that it can be referred to or added to at later points.

Commentary   If there is more than one trainer then it is a good idea for the trainers to fill out a sheet of their own. It saves time if the newsprint is ready sectioned off with borders. The formats shown on p. 75 are examples which would be suitable for three, four or five questions. Five questions are probably the maximum that can be tackled. You may wish to give examples, but if so remember there is a risk of leading the answers. It is possible to use unequal areas for the questions if you wish to indicate that some are more important than others, but this may appear manipulative.

List of questions

What I want from the course.
What I can offer the course.
My hopes.
My concerns.
One thing I hope won't happen.
One thing I hope will happen.
What my manager wants me to gain from the course.
One thing I want to know by the end of the course.
One skill I want to have by the end of the course.
How will I know that the course has been successful for me?
What my dream is (in the form of a picture).
Something I may do to jeopardize the team (for example, epileptic fit, sabotage).

Sample news print layouts

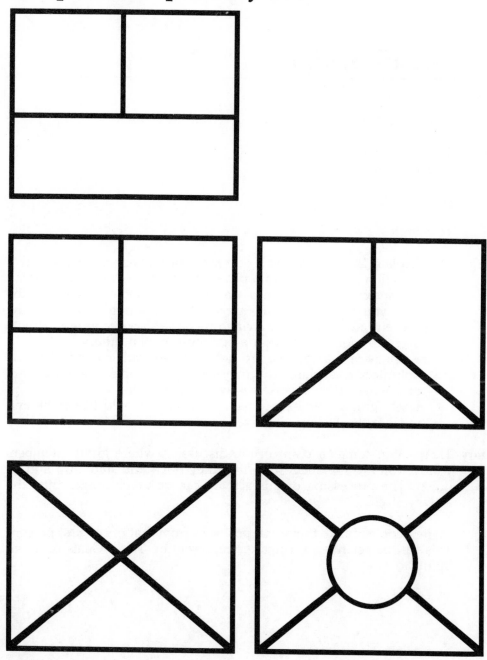

Figure 2

Group Sculpture

Summary   A sculpture represents aspects of group function.

Objectives   Team-building.
Self-disclosure.

Materials   None.

Timing   15 minutes.

Procedure
1. Explain that it is possible to represent any aspect of the way a situation is perceived in a physical way. One way is to position members of a group in a way that says something about the way you perceive them. Suggest that this might apply to the present group. Model moving one or two people around. Invite a group member to form a sculpture of the others.
2. Emphasize that people are not to move until moved. Ask the volunteer to explain why they have put people where they are and where they themselves would like to be.
3. Invite group members to say where they would like to be and explore the feelings involved.

Commentary   There often comes a point in the discussion where group members will respond to the suggestion that they break the statue up and sit down. The processing of this activity can be much longer than the activity itself.

Variation   Invite people to take their own positions from that of the first person. This can be relative to a marker representing Team Goals or Team Spirit.

Hand to Mouth

Summary   Imitating exercise with non-verbal distractions.

Objectives   Non-verbal communication.
Attention switching.

Materials   None.

Timing   Ten minutes.

Procedure   1.   Explain that you are going to give participants a series of instructions which you would like all of them to copy as fast as they can
2.   State the following actions as you do them:

– Put your hand to your nose;
– clap your hands;
– stand up;
– touch your shoulder;
– sit down;
– stamp your foot;
– cross your arms;
– put your hand to your mouth.

But while saying the last statement put your hand to your *nose*.
3.   Observe the number of participants who copy what you did rather than what you said.

Commentary   You may wish to add some theory about the importance of non-verbal communication.

Variation   Appoint some observers to the group before you start.

Here and Now

Summary   A game to limit the interference effects of reflective exercises.

Objectives   Attention switching (by restoring participants to the "here and now" after any reflective exercise that may have thrown up insights and reactions in them).

Materials   None.

Timing   Seven minutes.

Procedure

1. Form participants into pairs and ask them to designate themselves A and B. Invite the As to take the Bs through the procedure.
2. As spend one minute asking Bs questions that require them to think about where they are. They might be "how many feet are there in this room?", "Name three blue things in this room", "Name three fruits you have to peel" or "Spell your name backwards". After three questions ask your partner "Are you back in the Here and Now?" If not then ask three more questions.
3. Invite pairs to swap roles.

Commentary This is an important exercise for participants to be able to do but is quite hard to learn. The trainer should give a number of examples, different ones each time the exercise is carried out. Keeping the topic of the questions to naming three of something seems to be particularly effective for some reason. After a few sessions ask participants to "Here and Now" themselves. It is important for the trainer to be able to do this to him or herself.

Interviews

Summary   Introductions exercise swapping questions and getting them answered.

Objectives   Introductions.
Energizer.
Self-disclosure.

Materials   Pens.
Paper.

Timing   40 minutes (depends on group size).

Procedure   1.   Ask participants to form pairs with someone in the group whom they know *least well*.
2.   Ask participants to choose five questions that they would like to be asked by their partner in introducing them to the rest of the group – this being done by them disclosing the answers. They are to decide on their questions and then tell them to their partner.
3.   When the group has had time to do this, ask participants to choose another partner who they do not know well. Tell them to identify their original partner and then tell the new partner what the questions are. The new partner must then ask the first person those questions and find out what the answers are.
4.   When this has been done, have participants introduce the person to the rest of the group.

Commentary   This exercise is not practical for groups larger than 12.

Variation   If the group is much over 12 then at Stage 3 ask participants to approach the first person they see not talking to someone and to introduce them to the person whose answers they have ascertained.

Invisible Tug-of-War

Summary   A mimed tug-of-war.

Objectives Team-building.
Energizer.
Attention switching.

Materials   None.

Timing   10 minutes.

Procedure   1. Ask participants to form two teams and to position themselves at opposite ends of the room.
2. Ask the two teams to name themselves.
3. Get the two teams to play a tug-of-war, but without a rope. They are to make it as realistic as possible. The trainer gives the signal to start.
4. Each team will probably play the part of the winner. The trainer can explore why they do this in a discussion afterwards.

Variation   Invisible basketball also works well. Often there will be two balls at one time!

Just a Minute

Summary   An exercise to test knowledge of a topic by timed talking in a competitive situation.

Objectives   Attention switching.
Energizer.
Validation.

Materials   Whiteboard to score on and markers.
Stopwatch.
Bell or whistle for trainer.
Something for participants to make noises with (like whistles, bells).
Prepared list of cards with topics relating to the subjects of the course on them.
Scoring system set out on newsprint.

Timing   30 minutes.

Procedure   1. Explain that the objective of the exercise is to speak for one minute, without deviation, hesitation or repetition, on a topic suggested by the trainer. Participants can challenge one another (one point if correct, one point to the speaker if incorrect), and whoever speaks as the whistle goes gets another point. Bonus points to anyone who speaks for the whole minute.
2. Start with a trivial round on a topic suggested by the trainer (like "knees") and proceed to further rounds. Then do the real thing. Use suggestions for topics by the participants, and topics relating to the learning points of the training event.

Variations   1. Invite participants to suggest topics.
2. Have participants working in two teams.
3. **Just a Minuet** is a musical variation. Individuals (or teams) sing a well-known song, but when a word is repeated they must use a different word or expression each time. The challenger then continues until the minute is up. You may give teams lyric sheets, but it is still a difficult and enjoyable fun activity.

Knotty Problems

Summary   A physical management task.

Objectives   Verbal communication.
Energizer.

Materials   None

Timing   Ten minutes.

Procedure

1. Ask for four volunteers and place them on the outside of the rest of the group. Announce that these are the "Managers" and the rest are "Minions".
2. Instruct the Minions to hold hands in a circle facing outwards. On orders from the trainer they form a knot without breaking hands, weaving in and out of each other.
3. Ask the Managers to get them unknotted. They may not tell the Minions to let go of each others' hands. The Minions are zombies and do whatever they are told until they are told to stop doing it. Time the exercise.
4. Then put all participants into a knot in the same way and undertake to unknot them with hands behind the back/over the telephone. Do so by saying "untie yourselves".
5. Hold a discussion on what took place and how they felt about it. Ensure that Managers and Minions are both able to reflect on their experience.

Commentary   Note that Managers rarely confer with each other before starting.

Variations

1. Managers are not allowed to use non-verbal communication.
2. Managers have eyes closed.
3. This can be used as an energizer or a trust exercise by not appointing Managers and just asking the group to form and then dissolve the knot.

Labels

Summary   Identifying a label that cannot be seen.

Objectives   Attributions.
Team-building.
Non-verbal communication.
Feedback.

Materials   Prepared sticky labels.
Pens.

Timing   15 minutes.

Procedure
1. Hand out the sticky labels face down and ask each participant to put their label on the forehead of another person *without their seeing what the label says*.
2. Invite them to discuss where they are going for the annual works outing and ask them to react to each other as if they were the person named on the label.
3. In the main group find out if people were able to guess their labels, and how. Discuss the assumptions and attributions that were being made.

Commentary The labels chosen here are useful for a team-building exercise in that they will help members of an organization understand each other's roles. This game is a variation of **Amnesia** (p. 34) and is related to **On Your Face** (p. 101).

Variation   Use labels showing moods and feelings.

Suggestions for labels

I'm The Boss.
I write your annual report.
You write my annual report.
I'm 16 years old.

I've just moved here.
I'm an ET trainee.
I flirt.
I'm gay.
I'm pregnant.
I was demoted.
I retire soon.
I'm a working mother.
I'm the Personnel Officer.
I am recovering from a nervous breakdown.
I work from a wheelchair.
I am the only black here.
I'm an alcoholic.

Lies! Lies!

Summary   Self-disclosure with some people telling lies.

Objectives   Introductions.
                 Non-verbal communication.
                 Listening skills.

Materials   Copies of instruction sheets.

Timing   30 minutes.

Procedure

1. Hand out to participants copies of their instructions, which they are not to let anyone else see.
2. Tell the group that an unspecified number of members may not be telling the truth. They are not to reveal their suspicions until asked to do so.
3. After each person has spoken for two minutes invite group members to ask questions.
4. Initiate a discussion on who was telling the truth. Ask those who were deceitful to introduce themselves truthfully.

Variations

1. The discussion can centre on listening skills (questions) or on non-verbal signals of deceit. These stress signs can include loss of control below the waist (legs crossing and uncrossing), hand before mouth or in collar, tics, sweating, hesitation, blushing and dilation of pupils. But honest self-disclosure will be more stressful for some people than others.
2. Vary the number of group members as liars.
3. As a twist to an introductions exercise you can have *no* liars.

Lies! Lies! – Instruction sheet A

So that group members can get to know each other you'll be asked to talk about yourself for two minutes.

You should *not tell the truth*.
You might like to invent your life history, your beliefs, your family or your interests, or any combination of these. You can tell the truth about some things though. And please try to be consistent and credible in your lying.

After you have spoken you may be asked questions about your story. You are to try to make the others believe in you.

Some members will be telling the truth and others will be lying. Try to work out which is which, but don't reveal your suspicions until invited to by the trainer.

If you know someone in the group then try to let other members of the group speak about them before you do.

Lies! Lies! – Instruction sheet B

So that group members can get to know each other you'll be asked to talk about yourself for two minutes.

You should tell the truth.
You might like to talk about your life history, your beliefs, your family or your interests to whatever extent you want, but please do not be deceitful.

After you have spoken you may be asked questions about your story. You are to try to make the others believe in you.

Some members will be telling the truth and others will be lying. Try to work out which is which but don't reveal your suspicions until invited to by the trainer.

If you know someone in the group then try to let other members of the group speak about them before you do.

Listening Limbs

Summary   Non-verbal communication exercise using parts of the body.

Objective   Non-verbal communication.

Materials   Prepared cards with parts of the body written or drawn on them (such as arms, pointed finger, fists, hands, eyebrows, eyelashes, lips, feet, buttocks, neck, hair).

Timing   20 minutes.

Procedure
1. Introduce non-verbal communication and active listening as topics.
2. Hand out the cards to participants and ask individuals or couples to demonstrate to the rest of the group how to listen with that part of the body. Encourage them to be creative and to think of any way at all in which that part of the anatomy could be used. Allow three minutes to prepare in which you can circulate round the group.
3. Carry out a round of demonstrations.
4. Discuss in the main group what they have learned about non-verbal communication.

Variations
1. The demonstrations can be in pairs with the cards then being swapped.
2. You can add other NVC factors like "distance between people" and "pens".

Martians

Summary   A description exercise making minimal assumptions.

Objectives   Written communication (through exploring assumptions in verbal communication and stretching vocabulary).

Materials   Names of objects on cards (for example, egg whisk, bicycle, anglepoise lamp, shredded wheat, zip fastener, lobster, sundial, honey, pine cone).

Timing   20 minutes.

Procedure
1. Ask participants to form into groups who have to describe an object to the others. They have to assume that the others are Martians and may not have the same number of limbs as we do, or whether or not they sense the same things. They may even be super-intelligent beings and blue in colour.
2. Groups decide how to do this, and choose a speaker to describe the object on their behalf. The other group of Martians has to decide (in a suitably Martian way) what the object is, or draw it.

Commentary   The objects chosen are commonplace but hard to describe on account of structure, texture, etc. Bear this in mind when selecting objects.

Variation   The difference of the Martians can be specified; for instance, they cannot see but sense distance through radar.

Mind Scan

Summary   A method of testing assumptions about a person.

Objective   Attention switching. (The use of this activity at the end of role plays is described on p. 23.)
Attributions.
Team-building.

Materials   Chairs.

Timing   20 minutes or longer.

Procedure   1. Explain how a name from childhood can cause all kinds of irrational reactions. Instant likes and dislikes can often be based on irrational and unrecognized memories. These "hooks" can often be identified and overcome with a Mind Scan. Invite participants to form pairs. Partners take turns to be the subject or the scanner.
2. The subject asks "Who do I remind you of?" "What type of person do I remind you of?" The scanner then tries to answer this, taking as long as necessary. The mask can be used to help isolate separate physical features, but clothes, tone of voice, height, posture, way of walking might all be important. The questioner then replies with the name of a person or type of person.
3. The subject asks "Why do I remind you of . . . ?" "In what ways do I remind you of . . . ?" The subject then asks "Why else do I remind you of . . . ?" "In what other ways do I remind you of . . . ?" (The scanner thinks of all the ways possible.) The scanner replies truthfully.
4. The subject asks "Is there anything left unsaid to . . . ?" or "Imagine what you would really like to say to . . . ." The scanner then reacts, being aware of his/her feelings and of other times when s/he has felt like this.
5. Un-role by the subject asking "In what ways am I different to . . . ?" The scanner replies. The subject, if not sufficiently

un-roled, may ask "In what other ways am I unlike . . ." as often as necessary. The scanner ends with "you are not . . . You are (name)." The subject then says "I am not . . . I am (name)."

6. The pairs change over and change among themselves.

Commentary On a team-building course this game can be used to ensure that people are responding to one another in an accurate way. The element of ritual in the wording is deliberate and relates to the element of "exorcism" in the objective.

Variation A less structured way of carrying out this exercise is to ask pairs to think of who their partner does and does not remind them of, and then to discuss those qualities and the extent to which they are "owned" by either party.

Mirrors

Summary   Trust exercise in reflecting the actions of a partner.

Objectives   Trust.

Materials   None.

Timing   Five minutes.

Procedure
1. Form participants into pairs and ask them to face each other with their feet about two feet apart.
2. Ask them to slowly copy the movements of each other, without moving their feet.
3. As they build up trust suggest that they lean forwards with their hands together as if they are reflections of each other.
4. In a group discuss how they felt about the experience.

Commentary   This game requires enough trust to have been established for physical intimacy to be established. With all games in this category it is important that participants should not be coerced into taking part.

Variations
1. Have the whole group in a circle facing inwards with each person mirroring the person opposite them.
2. Have the whole group in a circle each one facing the back of the person to their right and mirroring them.

Mornington Crescent

Summary   Rule finding game.

Objectives   Non-verbal communication.
Energizer.

Materials   None.

Timing   Ten minutes.

Procedure

1. Explain "I am going to start a game in which you take it in turn to name streets of London. When someone has named a street I shall say 'yes' if it fits the rule that I am applying and 'no' if it does not. At any point you can try and guess what the rule is. If you guess wrongly then you drop out of the game."
2. As the game proceeds say "yes" or "no" as you please. Always precede a "yes" with an "um". Play until someone guessed the rule – making your ploy more obvious if it is not being guessed.
3. Discuss the observation skills that were being used.

Commentary   Ensure that your form of words does not imply that the rule is something to do with the word you choose (though most of the group will assume this).

Variations   The rule could simply relate, for example, to whether the players' legs are crossed or uncrossed when he or she says the word. In countries other than England the name of the city could be changed. This class of rule-guessing games includes those where there is no rule.

    The classic version of **Mornington Crescent** is rather different. It is a party game in which anyone can say any London street name and the only rule is that the first person who says "Mornington Crescent" wins. It is commonly played with a mix of people some of whom know and some of whom do not know the rules. This game was played regularly on the British radio panel game "I'm

Sorry I Haven't a Clue" and makes a good energizer if there are a few people in the group who know how to play it.

Mutual Introductions

Summary   Group introduction exercise.

Objectives   Introductions.

Materials   Pen and paper.

Timing   20 minutes for 12 people.

Procedure
1. Ask participants to work in pairs, where possible not known to each other, and label themselves A and B.
2. Inform them that A has four minutes in which to interview B about his or her life and interests. A may take notes. Then they should swap roles.
3. In the main group ask participants to introduce their partners and introduce each other to the main group.

Variations
1. Give participants some specific questions to which you would like answers. Leave some open ended, (for example, "three things you can't tell by looking at them", "three roles that are important to them in their life"). You can include course expectations and training experience.
2. Encourage participants to discuss the results of an earlier exercise in pairs.

Name Plate Shuffle

Summary   Partners ascertain why they have been regrouped.

Objectives   Attention switching.
Energizer.
Introductions.
Self-disclosure.

Materials   Name plates.

Timing   15 minutes.

Procedure

1. While the group are out of the room re-arrange their name plates so that they are in groups of unequal sizes. Do so randomly or to separate out cliques within the group if that is something you wish to do.
2. Ask them to hold a buzz group* session (explaining what that is if necessary) on why they have been put together. Deflect any attempt to find out the answer from you.
3. Bring the groups together and ask what they thought of the exercise and what they have found out about each other.

Commentary This a good "first break" exercise for a training event where you wish to establish a highly participative culture early on.

*Adams (1974) and Eitington (1989) contain good accounts of what buzz groups are and how to use them.

Number Crunches

Summary   Group members form formations of certain numbers as requested.

Objectives   Team-building (exploring group identity).
Energizer and attention switching.

Materials   None.

Timing   20 minutes.

Procedure   1. Explain that you will call out numbers into which the group
has to form. This must be done in silence and participants
cannot be questioned as to which group they have joined. They
may give non-verbal signals to help create their group or stop
it getting too big. Nobody can be stopped from joining or
leaving a group. When someone is "out" they go to the side
of the room.
2. Start off with numbers into which the group can be divided
without anyone being left out and then move to numbers which
will leave one person out. Include "singles" every now and
again, for which people space themselves out over the room.
If one person makes a group too large by joining it then keep
calling until the right number is formed. The caller can wave
his/her arms around or be sarcastic, but it is for the participants
to move. Keep calling until you are down to the last three.
3. Discuss why they acted the way they did. Who opted out and
when. Who felt rejected and how did they know? Who did the
rejecting?

Commentary   Some numbers do not break up. If you have eight people left and
call "a four and a three" then two fours may form and each will
regard itself as "the real four". Alternatively, point out the phenom-
enon and then re-call a different number.

Variation   Play the game a second time asking the first person out to be caller.
The trainer takes part and stays put (not moving or going out when

not part of a group). The learning point here is that "everyone knew where I stood".

One Pound Auction

Summary   Participants bid for a £1 coin.

Objectives   Team-building.
Decision making.
Non-verbal communication.
Assertiveness.
Listening skills.

Materials   Chairs.

Timing   15 minutes.

Procedure
1. Form participants into a tight circle of chairs so that their fingers would touch if their arms were fully outstretched. Announce that you are going to hold a mock auction for a £1 coin, only you would like the participants to behave as though you were really auctioning it.
2. Explain that participants will have to pay the value of their bid. Encourage everyone to join in, emphasizing that they will not be losing anything in reality.
3. Proceed to solicit bids. Use arm gestures to "bring in" people and a lot of eye contact and enthusiasm. When the bidding falters point out that participants have already lost the value of their bid and so they might just as well continue. Once bids are past 99 pence this will not be difficult.
4. Discuss the procedure followed. How did people decide what risks to take? How was the trainer able to solicit bids for so long?

Commentary   The success of this game depends upon the non-verbal skills of the trainer in securing the enthusiasm of the group. A trainer who has not tried the game for him or herself should see it done well before attempting it.

Variations   If listening skills are most important then use a form of words like "if the first person bids a penny and the second person bids two pence and then nobody bids at all then the second person gets the coin." This can be used to illustrate how the group – had they listened and acted as one – could have secured the coin for the group and divided it among themselves. If assertiveness is the teaching point then the discussion should bring out the value of being submissive in some circumstances.

On Your Face

Summary   Identification of labels through the responses they evoke.

Objectives   Energizer.
Non-verbal communication.
Attributions.

Materials   Marker pens.
Prepared headbands (examples given below). Two strips of paper or card of A4 length taped together will fit an average head.

Timing   20 minutes.

Procedure   1. Form participants into pairs, excluding the trainers. Explain that you are going to put a headband onto each participant which will offer instructions on how that person is to be treated by others. Do so. They should not get the chance to see their own headbands.
2. Ask pairs to find as many areas of common interest as they can in ten minutes, reacting to each other as though the labels were true.
3. After ten minutes stop the discussion and, as a group, talk about how people managed to guess what was on their headband. Ask them for parallels from their own experience. How might such messages be transmitted? Are they aware of any such messages that they give to other people?

Commentary   This activity is related to **Amnesia** (p. 34) and **Labels** (p. 83). It can also be used to explore the internal "voices" that seem to push people into behaving in certain ways. (Stewart and Joines 1987, chapter 16 describe a transactional analysis approach to this idea.)

Variations   1. Rather than talking in pairs, participants can form a group and discuss any topic in that context.
2. Blank headbands can be handed out and participants asked to fill them out and put them on someone else's head. There is a

101

risk in that case that some of the descriptions might be offensive.

3. One headband (or more) could be left blank to show how people can project their own feelings.
4. Another task for the pairs is trying to persuade that person to go to a restaurant/pub/club of your choice.

Possible headbands

Reject me.   Patronize me.
Be impressed by me.   Flatter me.
Admire me.   Hate me.
Despise me.   Ignore me.
Obey me.   Seduce me.
Feel sorry for me.   Impress me.
Distrust me.   Lie to me.

Pickpockets

Summary   Creativity exercise using the contents of people's pockets.

Objectives   Creativity.
Team-building.
Problem solving.
Trainer training.

Materials   Pens.
Paper.

Timing   45 minutes.

Procedure   1. Define an area in which creativity is going to be assessed (for instance, solving a management problem). Ask one group member or the whole group to empty their pockets.
2. Put all the items in a heap. Ask the group to divide into pairs and give them one object. Invite them to devise a solution using that object to inspire them in any way they wish.
3. Bring the pairs together and discuss what solutions they devised, making the groups progressively larger.

Commentary Sometimes a pair will have a real block, in which case you may allow them to exchange their object. A better way might be to suggest that they think of similes: for example, by listing the qualities of the object and then asking themselves in what way is the problem like or unlike the object. It is important to allow plenty of time for the discussion stage.

Variations   1. Have a box of objects to hand (toys, etc.).
2. Use picture postcards or pictures from magazines.

Possibilities

Summary   Investigation of unconscious messages that constrain our attitude towards possible courses of action.

Objectives   Self-disclosure.

Materials   Pens.
Paper.

Timing   One hour.

Procedure   1.   Ask participants to spend ten minutes writing down statements starting with the words "I must . . ." or "I have to . . . " – things that they feel that they have to do for other people. They can be either positive or negative (such as "Be feminine", "Do not make the first move", "Ask for what I want", "Seem vulnerable").

2.   Ask them to consider their lists and add "Or else . . ." statements to them – what they think the consequences would be of *not* acting in that way (such as "Others might not understand my point", "Others might take advantage of me", "Others might like me", "I'll be made fun of").

3.   Ask participants to form into pairs and to help each other to clarify their lists. Ask them to consider how they might replace their statements with others beginning "I choose to . . ." and "I want to . . ." Also ask them to think about the ones that they do not change. How important are they?

4.   Discuss in the full group what they have learned about themselves and the possibilities which they allow themselves to consider. If necessary offer to go into the theory of script and drivers (Stewart and Joines 1987, offer a good general account, while Dainow and Bailey 1988, creatively apply them to stress management).

Commentary   This activity requires a fairly high degree of trust from group members, and therefore might be more appropriate in the later stages of a course.

Variation   At Stage 2 invite participants to delete all but the three most important messages.

Problems Without Words

Summary   Group problem solving exercise in which words are not used.

Objectives   Team-building.
Non-verbal communication.
Problem solving.

Materials   Newsprint and many coloured pencils.

Timing   Three hours.

Procedure   1.   Explain that the group will be looking at problems and solutions
in a defined area (say what it is) and that this will be done in
collective silence. From the start of the exercise until its con-
clusion, everyone will stay together except for visiting the lavatory. Start on a signal from a participant. The exercise works
well if started during a joint meal and can be carried on going
out on a walk where it can "free up" child-like (but not childish)
reactions and spontaneity.
2.   On returning to the course room, hand out sheets of paper and
non-verbally ask participants to write down problems in the
area they have decided to work on. Sheets can be pre-prepared
with subject areas on them. Get them to change pens and
sheets. Carry on until each person has worked on three or four
different sheets. Then do the same working on answers and
encouraging them to comment on each other's sheets.
3.   End by encouraging participants to form a circle. The trainer
should not be the first one to speak.

Commentary **Silent Meal/Silent Walk** (p. 115) contains guidance on the first part
of this game. It is important to ensure that participants know exactly
what they will be doing as it is difficult to clarify the working of the
exercise while it is taking place. Processing the problems/solutions
first and the silent activity afterwards ensures that there is a focus
on the problem. Someone (a group member rather than a trainer)
will have to take the sheets away and distil them. Although this
task is not difficult, it can be time consuming.

Re-Inventing the Wheel

Summary   Participants invent new activities to fit old titles.

Objective   Creativity.

Materials   Paper and pens may be required.
Pro-forma (given on the following page).
List of games (see pp. 149).

Timing   45 minutes.

Procedure   1. Divide participants into pairs and give them the list of titles of games (see p. 149) and the pro-forma.
2. Tell them to put any familiar one out of their mind and to pick one that they have not used. Invite them to invent a training game to fit the title and to describe it on the pro-forma.
3. The games are described and may be played. The trainer then reveals the real nature of the activities if asked and explains those that have been made up.

Commentary Appendix 1 contains a self-instruction programme for trainers into which this activity can be fitted in a training course.

Variation   Substitute sports or board games as the activity to be designed.

Summary

Materials

Timing

Objectives

Procedure

Commentary

RSVP

Summary   Exercise exploring tone by the writing of party invitations.

Objectives   Written communication (specifically to explore the nature of written style and the fact that it consists of far more than "formal/informal").

Materials   Whiteboard.
Prepared cards with roles of people (for example, Member of Parliament, priest/rabbi, ex-boy or girlfriend (whom you would rather did not come), next-door neighbour, best friend, boss, five year old child, Secretary of State, Managing Director, mother, someone you were at school with).
Paper and pens.

Timing   15 minutes.

Procedure
1. Hand out the cards (one to each person) and describe an end of course party. It may be useful to have the details on the board (date, time and duration, place, whether food and drink is provided, whether it is fancy dress, etc.).
2. Ask participants to rough out an invitation to the party to the person on their card.
3. When they've read them out ask what style they thought it was in. Ask others participants for names of styles that might be appropriate. Write up the styles as they emerge, and end by identifying which of them you might use in official correspondence.

Commentary   In a large group it may not be necessary or worthwhile to involve each person. Instead take three or four answers from named individuals and then ask who has drafts in other tones and put them up. This game should be conducted briskly or people will spend too much time agonizing over their drafts.

Rude Aerobics

Summary   Energizer naming parts of the body.

Objectives   Attention switcher.
Energizer.

Materials   Dance music and a music player.

Timing   Ten minutes.

Procedure
1. Introduce the activity as an aerobic loosening exercise. Start the music and encourage the participants to move around and loosen up.
2. Ask subjects to move around more energetically, feeling their heads, ears, noses, etc., and greeting them, for example, "hello nose", "good morning hair", etc.).
3. Gradually make the parts of the body more intimate (for example, "good morning, balls", "how are you doing today, nipples?", "hello, cock").

Commentary It is useful to have a trainer of each sex participating in this exercise. This is a very high-risk activity, but on more than one occasion has loosened up a group that regarded participative training as "beneath them" – by presenting them with an exercise that they could not possibly take seriously.

Rules of the Game

Summary   Inventing games and guessing what they are.

Objectives   Creativity.

Materials   Paper and pens may be required.
List of exercises.

Timing   One and a half hours.

Procedure
1. Divide participants into groups and ask them to invent a game that involves at least two members of the group. It can have as few or as many rules as the group wishes, but these must be written down. The list of titles of games from **Reinventing the Wheel** (p. 107) can be given out to encourage people to think, but if should not be necessary.
2. When the groups are ready, ask them to play their game. The other groups have the task of guessing the rules from seeing the game played.

Variation   Trainers may be asked to devise an energizer or a learning activity either on any topic or on a specific theme (for instance, for use on a management course). These can be collected in, set out in the format of these notes and given to all participants later in the course.

Sabotage

Summary   Sabotage of discussion by a third party.

Objectives   Sabotage.
                 Assertiveness.

Materials   Chairs.

Timing   20 minutes.

Procedure   1. Ask participants to form into groups of three and to label them-selves A, B and C. (The trainer can be a participant or a roving saboteur as needed for the numbers.)
                 2. Invite them to take the roles of Speaker (A), Listener (B) (sitting face to face) and (C) Saboteur (seated perpendicularly between them). The Speaker is to speak on a topic for three minutes. The Listener is to listen without speaking and the Saboteur is to stop the flow of communication. The Listener and Speaker are to allow themselves to be distracted. After three minutes rotate the roles.
                 3. Rotate the roles twice and then lead into a discussion of how it felt to interrupt and to be interrupted, and how it related to power.

Commentary   This activity helps to examine the issue of sabotage openly during the course, which might be difficult otherwise. It also provides a useful label based on experience if anyone in the group should try sabotage later. At a deeper level, participants can explore (perhaps in pairs) when they have left in exclusion groups, either as the person excluded or as the person conspiring to exclude. As a roving Saboteur the trainer can involve other Saboteurs and cause a great deal of good natured interference.

Variation   Second time around, the speakers and listeners can be invited to try and involve the saboteur. Third time around, the listener can also speak.

Selves and Possibilities

Summary   Comparison of self in different circumstances with ideal self.

Objectives   Self-development.
Self-disclosure.
Team-building.
Action planning.

Materials   Blank cards (six per person).
Pens.

Timing   25 minutes.

Procedure
1. Distribute the cards to participants individually.
2. Explain that you are going to ask them to think about themselves in different situations. Ask them to think of words to describe "What I am like when I am at work". Two or three adjectives are all that is required.
3. Then do them same for "What I am like when I am at home", and "What I am like when I am by myself".
4. Then do the same for "What I would like to be when I am at work", "What I would like to be when I am at home", and "What I would like to be when I am by myself".
5. Invite them to discuss in pairs what the differences are between their present and the ideal state, and what might be the best way of reconciling the two.
6. Invite them to share anything they wish with the main group.

Commentary The approach used here is based on that of Carl Rogers to counselling, which was to consider the difference between the self and the ideal self (Rogers 1951). The trainer interested in adding a short input session on this approach could consult Hampden-Turner (1981).

Variations
1. Invite participants to close their eyes and imagine themselves in the various states.

2. Choose all work-related situations (for example, "What I am like as a line manager", "What I would like to be when I am being managed by others").

3. Carry out the exercise at the start and at the end of the course, and ask participants to look at the differences.

4. At Stage 5, place more emphasis on pairs comparing the different ideal states, present states, and the differences between them.

Silent Meal/Silent Walk

Summary   Group exercise in which words are not used.

Objectives Team-building.
Non-verbal skills.

Materials   A meal break and access to outdoors.

Timing   90 minutes.

Procedure
1. Suggest to participants that in working teams group members often become so task-oriented that they may fail to respond to each other as individuals. Introduce an exercise to take them through their lunch break which will attempt to restore that sensitivity.
2. Explain that apart from visits to the lavatory, the group will stay together at all times for the next 90 minutes. During that time they *should not speak at all*. They are not to write messages to each other either. Communication should be non-verbal as well as non-vocal. You hope, however, that they will enjoy the time that they are spending together. Encourage them to think about their experiences and their feelings during that time. Over that period there will be a joint meal and the group can then go out for a walk. Start on a signal from any group member.
3. Take the group through their meal and walk, modelling silence throughout.
4. When in the course room wait for the silence to end. The trainer should not be the first person to speak. Initiate a discussion on their feelings and their experiences. How did they feel about themselves? Did they enjoy it? How did they think that they were perceived by other people? What did they learn about themselves and the way that they can operate as a group?

Commentary Ensure that participants know exactly what they will be doing, as it is difficult to clarify the working of the exercise while it is taking place. Participants will often record heightened sensations such as taste during the meal. They may hold hands during their walk. The trainer will have to keep an eye out for the group during the walk as the apparent playfulness of the group may attract unwanted attention from others. The group's activities should not be of such a nature that any problems are caused. The perceptions of others are important to be aware of. Often it will take groups at other tables during the meal some while to work out what is happening, though they may realize that "something is up".

Variations   Other activities can be included such as outdoor or indoor games and recreations, as long as they do not involve reading and will not inhibit eye contact. **Problems Without Words** (p. 106) is a development of this activity.

Statue Stop

Summary   Energizer in which participants mould one another into shapes.

Objectives   Energizer.
Attention switching.

Materials   None.

Timing   12 minutes.

Procedure
1. Form the group into two concentric circles with members facing each other. Those on the outer circle are sculptors, and those on the inside are the raw material.
2. Invite the sculptors to form the material into a shape that is pleasing to them.
3. Ask the sculptors to move round one space clockwise and to look at the sculpture facing them, changing it if they wish. Continue until the outer circle has been all the way round.

Variations
1. Have participants scattered across the room in pairs, one partner then being the sculptor and the sculptors circulating round the room.
2. Reverse the roles at the end of the exercise.

Stamps

Summary   An exchange of self-perceptions.

Objectives   Self-disclosure.
Team-building.

Materials   Prepared sticky labels (12 per person).
Pens.

Timing   30 minutes.

Procedure
1. Hand out the labels and pens. The labels should have been prepared with the words "I am" printed on them. Ask participants to divide them into two piles and to write six things they *like* about themselves and six things they *do not like* about themselves. They are not to worry if they cannot think of enough, and they will not have to disclose anything they do not want to.
2. Divide the group into threes and invite them to discuss their labels. They might wish to consider the balance of positives and negatives, where the labels have come from, and the extent to which there is any overlap in the labels they have.
3. Bring the whole group together and invite the triads to share what they have learned from the exercise.

Commentary   You may wish to raise some of the psychological work on labelling during the discussion (Stewart and Joines 1987).

Time Lapse

Summary   A circle energizer in which participants imitate each other.

Objectives   Energizer.
Attention switching.

Materials   None.

Timing   Two minutes and upwards.

Procedure
1. Form participants into a circle and ask for a volunteer.
2. Explain that the volunteer is the Controller and will initiate an action that will be imitated by all the participants round the circle. Whoever starts chooses the direction and chooses the time lapse between imitations (for example, if s/he calls "two" then the lapse is two seconds). The "action" passes round the group until it reaches the initiator, where it ends unless s/he decides to sponsor it again. Any player can become Controller at any time by calling a new time and action (or just a new time and the same action). *The old action does not lapse until it reaches its originator again.*
3. Demonstrate, ask if clarification is needed, and then proceed with the game.

Commentary This game usually ends with as many actions as there are participants.

Variation   The action can be repeating a word or sentence or a song as well as a physical action.

Time Lines

Summary   Mapping of perception of one's life.

Objectives   Team-building.
Self-perception.

Materials   Newsprint.
Pens.

Timing   20 minutes.

Procedure   1.   Ask what is the earliest date at which you could arrange an
appointment with the group members *on any day of the week*.
Assess the differences by establishing ranges, "one day?". "two
days?". . . . Introduce the concept of "time lines", which are
like antennae which we use to project ourselves into the future.
The length and strength of people's time lines will differ.
2.   Ask participants to draw their time lines in any way they wish
and then invite them to discuss them in pairs. Draw out any
points people wish to disclose in the main group.

Variation   Time maps could be used instead, in which group members map
out the important stages of their life, moving from the past through
to the future in stages.

Tones of Voice

Summary   Exercise in identifying tones of voice.

Objectives Written communication.
Energizer.
Attention switching.
Non-verbal communication.

Materials   Prepared slips of paper (see below).
Prepared sheet of paper (see below).

Timing   15 minutes.

Procedure   1. Introduce the subject of tone and the way that it can affect communication. Ask for some examples of the styles that something might be said in, and the assumptions that can be based on tones of voice. Write down examples on slips of paper; for example,

- police officer reading a statement in court
- politician giving a speech
- parent reading a bedtime story
- someone who is bored to tears
- drowning person crying for help
- speaking full of innuendo and double meaning

2. Allocate the slips of paper around the group so that participants do not know what the others have, and give them a passage to read in that way. The others have to guess what the tone is.
3. Process by discussing *how* tone is put into speech, what it means and (if appropriate) how it can be done in writing.

Commentary This leads into **RSVP** very well if written communication is the topic under discussion. I have found that the use of a "neutral" passage (like a recipe, assembly instructions) is better than something for which there is a natural tone (like an extract from Shakespeare). This also introduces humour into the activity.

Variations

1. Different passages can be used for each person.
2. For a shorter version of the game the tones or styles can be written out beforehand.

Truth Option

Summary   Participants can either admit that they belong to a certain category or not.

Objectives   Self-disclosure.
Energizer.
Action planning.
Validation.

Materials   A ring of chairs.

Timing   Ten minutes.

Procedure
1. Form the participants into a circle with yourself in the centre.
2. Explain that the person in the middle is "it" and must request all those in a category to stand up (for example, "everyone who is wearing contact lenses stand up"). Participants may lie, either by standing or remaining seated, and nobody may question anyone else's right to do so. Having stood up, nobody can sit in the seat that they themselves vacated. The one without a seat is "it" for the next round.
3. Questions that fail can be reversed (for instance, "Anyone who is happy with this course stand up [no response] . . . anyone with any concerns about the course stand up"). There is also a "truth supplementary" (that is, "will anyone who lied on the last question stand up"). Feeling directives like "All who were embarrassed by the last question stand up" can be asked.
4. Demonstrate, ask if clarification is needed, and then proceed with the game.

Commentary   The exercise allows self-disclosure, but also allows participants to lie either positively or negatively. In practice it is very difficult to see who is standing and sitting if you are too, and this also encourages honesty. The questions can become very personal. By ensuring s/he is "it" fairly often, the trainer can extend or model types of question (like reflective, feeling, truth supplementaries). This is good as a feedback exercise to get a feel for the way in which to handle a later session, or where to take the group next. If this is being used as a feedback exercise then the trainer will ensure that s/he is "it" fairly often.

Variation   In a milder form this exercise can be used as an energizer. In this version, keep the sample questions non-intimate and end the exercise sooner.

Ugly Sisters

Summary   Energizer based on exchanging shoes.

Objectives   Energizer.
Attention switcher.

Materials   None.

Timing   Ten minutes.

Procedure   1. Invite all participants to take off their shoes and put them into a heap.
2. Ask them to take two shoes out with their eyes closed and put them on.
3. Ask them to attempt to form into a line so that the pairs of shoes are next to each other.

Commentary This activity is suitable for groups of between six and 12 participants.

Variations   Ask participants to keep one shoe on and pick one shoe out of the pile. Allow them to put the shoes on their hands if they wish.

Voluntaries

Summary   An exploration of why participants volunteer for an unspecified activity.

Objectives   Assertiveness.
Motivation.
Team-building.

Materials   None.

Timing   20 minutes.

Procedure
1. Ask for volunteers for "an interesting activity". The number sought should be about half the group. Wait until the appropriate number of people have volunteered.
2. Ask the volunteers to carry out an activity, either individually or as a group. The nature of the activity is unimportant (for instance, collectively carrying a large bowl of water to the corners of the room, individually taking off their wristwatches and putting them on the other arm).
3. Form buzz groups including the volunteers to consider the exercise so far and the way they felt about volunteering or not volunteering. These feelings can be explored in the main group.

Commentary This is a good way to introduce the topic of process discussion to a group.

War of Words

Summary   Participants take and exchange viewpoints in an argument.

Ojectives   Non-verbal communication.
                Attention switching.

Materials   None.

Timing   20 minutes.

Procedure
1. Ask participants to form pairs and choose a topic on which they will talk.
2. Say that for the purposes of the exercise one of them will argue in favour of one point of view and the other will oppose it. Stress that it does not matter if in reality they both hold the same view. They are to take opposing views and do all they can to persuade the other to change his/her mind.
3. Explain that at a signal they will swap roles.
4. After going through the exercise, discuss what people have learned about their views and about themselves.

Commentary Those who have started arguing against their original view can have difficulty in reverting to it. There is evidence that the process of opposition encourages participants to gather more evidence for their own views, and as a result on occasions to change them.

Variation   Participants can be lined up in two rows before being asked to start their argument and then, on a signal, to change roles. This will enable them to contribute some observations on each other's non-verbal behaviour, but it will make for a noisy session.

Waxworks

Summary   Exercise in which participants do not try to communicate with each other.

Objectives   Non-verbal communication.

Materials   None.

Timing   20 minutes.

Procedure

1. Ask participants to form into pairs, label themselves A and B and sit opposite one another. Ask the As to spend three minutes (which you will time) not communicating with their partners.
2. The Bs are to note all the non-verbal signals coming from the As (eye contact, breathing, muscle tension, and so on). Suggest that they might try to synchronize their breathing with that of their partners.
3. After that, ask the pairs to exchange roles.
4. Invite the pairs to discuss what they felt about the exercise and what they discovered about themselves, and then to share anything they wish with the main group.

Commentary   A point that often emerges is that it is actually very hard not to receive signals from a person and to perceive them as a waxwork.

Variation   Exchange partners a few times before going on to the discussion stage.

What'll be my Line?

Summary   One participant guesses for what job s/he is being interviewed.

Objectives   Energizer.
Attributions.
Verbal communication.

Materials   None.

Timing   20 minutes.

Procedure
1. Ask for a volunteer, who must leave the room and then come back and "be interviewed for a job". His or her task is to secure the job.
2. Remaining participants select an occupation of an unusual character (such as an astronaut, a cardinal, a greetings card verse writer, a private detective, a sewer cleaner, a bodyguard, a tree surgeon, a public house signwriter), and role play an interviewing panel which will interview the other person as a candidate *without revealing the nature of the job*. Candidates continue until they guess the nature of the job.
4. In discussion consider the questions that were most effective, and the assumptions that were being made about the job.

Wheel of Experience

Summary   An experience sharing exercise.

Objectives   Team-building.
Problem solving.

Materials   Pens and paper.
Chairs.

Timing   One hour.

Procedure
1. Ask participants to describe in two sentences a problem that they have, and to write it down. Encourage consideration of the fact that problems are challenges, and insist that it be expressed in the form "My challenge is. . . ." Introduce the concept of an experience exchange. The emphasis is not "what I would do . . .", but "in my experience . . ." A good example is baking a cake, where what someone might do could well be slightly different from the "official" recipe.
2. Ask the group to divide themselves into two equal groups. Then form them into two concentric circles, inner facing out and outer facing in, on chairs. The inner circle are "consultants" and the outer "clients". Consultants need no paper or pen.
3. Explain that clients should spend one minute explaining their challenge. If they finish early the consultant can ask clarification questions or begin responding. Otherwise there are two minutes for the consultant to respond, beginning "in my experience..", and if s/he has no experience to say so and then stop. After three minutes a short time will be allowed for the clients to take notes using the papers and pens provided, to thank their consultant, and to move clockwise. This will continue until the consultants have gone right around the circle.
4. Ask if clarification is needed and then proceed.
5. When all consultants and clients have met then, if you have time, change roles and repeat. If not then discuss what participants learned from the experience and how they feel about it.

Commentary In processing this exercise ask how the nature of the questions changed, and how many different answers the clients got. Do a circle feedback for client roles first for each person, and after that for being a consultant. If time is short it is not crucial that the clients see all the consultants.

Variation Ask participants to bring problems with them. These can be costed (for example, "a problem worth £2,000").

Whirlpool

Summary   Each person tries to get as close as possible to one person and as far as possible from another.

Objectives   Energizer.
Attention switcher.

Materials   None.

Timing   Five minutes.

Procedure
1. Ask each participant to silently choose one person to be their "A" and another to be their "B".
2. Then explain that the object is to get as close as possible to their A and as far as possible from their B, that is, to keep their A between themselves and their B.
3. If no clarification is necessary then proceed with the game.

Commentary This is an exceptionally lively and tiring energizing activity. Its name refers to the swirling pattern of participants that usually results.

Whispers

Summary   Listening exercise.

Objectives   Listening skills.

Materials   None.

Timing   Ten minutes, plus five minutes per participant.

Procedure   1. Explain that you are going to ask all apart from one person to
                       leave the room and that you will then tell something to the
                       remaining person. You will then ask them to repeat what they
                       have heard to another person and so forth until the whole
                       group have been brought in.
                   2. Then tell a story which could be the one used for **Are You
                       Sitting Comfortably** (p. 39), though it may have to be a little
                       shorter.
                   3. At the end ask participants to write down how the story
                       changed from the version that they heard. What was left out,
                       what was added and what was changed?
                   4. Tell the story again to the whole group and lead a discussion
                       on the changes that have taken place.

Commentary During the discussion you may wish to refer to the work of Bartlett
                (1932) on memory, and the systematic way in which it can be dis-
                torted.

Variation   You can take a passage from a paper or magazine (make sure that
                   it is unfamiliar to the participants).

Who's Who?

Summary   Game in which partners identify each other.

Objectives   Trust.

Materials   None.

Timing   15 minutes.

Procedure
1. The participants should form pairs.
2. Ask them to spend time with their partners so that they will be able to identify them later. Then ask them to mill round the room.
3. Participants should now find their partners with their eyes closed and without speaking – only using touch.
4. Discuss how they managed to turn their visual impression into tactile form.

Commentary This game requires enough trust to have been established between the participants to make physical contact possible. This should not be a problem, but make sure that the contract is emphasized and that people do not feel that they have to participate if they are uneasy about doing so.

Variation   The two parts of the exercise can be separated in time.

Wibble-Wobble

Summary   Energizer in which participants take it in turn to say "wibble" or "wobble".

Objectives   Energizer.
Attention switcher.

Materials   None.

Timing   Seven minutes.

Procedure   1. Form participants into a circle and explain the following rules:

(a) Only speak when you are spoken to.
(b) Speak either to the person on your left or your right, whichever you wish.
(c) If you speak to the person on your right say "wibble".
(d) If you speak to the person on your left say "wobble".
(e) Speak as soon as possible after you have been spoken to.

2. Play the game as fast as you can.

Commentary   This is a lively energizer which works very well in loosening up a group. It is also successful with people who have a visual or mobility disability.

Will to Live

Summary   Exercise simulating writing a will.

Objectives   Self-disclosure.
Self-perception.

Materials   Prepared paper printed at the start: "I —- being of sound mind hereby revoke all wills and testaments made by me" and ending "Signed —- and dated —-".
Pens.
Paper.

Timing   40 minutes.

Procedure

1. Hand out the prepared sheets and explain that you are going to give group members an opportunity to do something they may never have done before – write their will.
2. Explain that this will be a will of personal qualities (whether good or bad) rather than material possessions. You will allow 15 minutes for participants to make their wills – leaving all the personal qualities to the person who will most benefit from them. Make it clear that they will not have to share anything they write with anyone else.
3. Invite participants to form pairs and discuss the qualities that they found, and how they decided who to allocate them to. Also, what (of any) qualities were not allocated to anybody. Allow ten minutes.
4. In the same pairs ask group members to discuss how they might give those qualities to that person *before* they die. Allow ten minutes for this.
5. Allow a general discussion of what people have learned about themselves from the exercise, but do not encourage self-disclosure further than that which is forthcoming from the group.

Commentary As a light ending you may suggest that group members do *not* have the wills witnessed or they will be legally binding!

Variation   In a team-building exercise the bequests could have to be to other members of the group, and then there could be more open sharing.

Word Search

Summary   Establishing connections between the meanings of words.

Objectives   Attributions.
Written communication.

Materials   As large a variety of dictionaries as possible (such as the Concise Oxford, Chambers' 20th Century, Longman's, Webster's Collegiate, an etymological dictionary).
Pens and flipchart paper.
Overhead transparency of a dictionary page (optional).

Timing   One hour.

Procedure
1. Brainstorm a list of appropriate words. For an equal opportunities course, for example, these might be colloquial and "official" words for people of different races, sexes, sexualities and disabilities. Put each set up on a separate sheet so that they can be distributed among syndicates.
2. Introduce the subject of studying the meanings and the origins of words. Use an overhead transparency of a dictionary to show where the origin and the records of early usage are.
3. Ask the participants to form groups and give them the lists. Give them a brief to spend 20 minutes looking at the meanings of the words on their lists in the different dictionaries, compare them to what they *thought* the meanings were, and to look at which are the older and the newer usages and what the relationships are between them.
4. In a discussion review what the groups have discovered about the way in which language is constructed and used.

Commentary   Some time with a thesaurus before the start of the session will give you an idea of some terms you may wish to use as "starters" to get the groups going. Participants can be surprised by discovering the meanings of words that they thought they knew, like "esquire" and "promiscuous".

Variation   The lists can be created in groups and can then be swapped for the second part of the exercise.

You Spy

Summary   Energizer reversal of **I Spy**.

Objectives   Energizer.
Attention switching.

Materials   None.

Timing   Five minutes.

Procedure
1. Ask the group to work in pairs, one member to start. The starter says "you spy with your little eye something beginning with . . ." The second person has to think of something starting with that letter. Then swap roles. The same letter cannot be used twice.
2. In a second round repeat the exercise, but here the pair should aim to alternate as many times as possible during the minute.

Commentary   Participants may make the exercise hard or easy for their partner. Explore the reasons for this.

140

Appendix: How to devise games

Learning objectives

After reading this Appendix and carrying out the activities in it, readers should:

- Understand the nature of creativity;
- Have developed more flexible ways of thinking about achieving training objectives;
- Have devised variations on an existing training game;
- Have designed and developed a new training game.

The programme consists of about six hours of work and thinking.

Activity 1: What is creativity?

Many people have different ideas of what creativity is. Write down yours and check it with three different dictionaries. Then think about the following questions:

- How do the definitions square with each other?
- How do they relate to yours?
- Is being creative the same as being original?

Creativity versus originality

Many people confuse creativity with originality. It is not necessary to rack your brains trying to think thoughts that have never been thought before to show creativity of thought. When he wrote his three famous papers in 1905, Einstein did not have a laboratory and was unable to conduct any experiments. What he did do was to bring together the findings of other people and make connections that nobody else had seen. As trainers we are often in the business of making connections and encouraging others to do so. This takes us a long way towards being creative.

A working definition of creativity

One way of defining creativity might be in operational terms – *having the most effective game possible to meet your chosen training objectives.* Would this satisfy you as an objective for the purposes of this chapter? If so then read on.

Activity 2: What it is to be creative

Consider the following list of occupations. To what extent do you think that it would be reasonable to say "Pat is a creative *x*" of that occupational category? Put your answers into three columns of DEFINITELY CREATIVE, POSSIBLY CREATIVE and UNCREATIVE.

List of occupations

Lumberjack	Monarch	Flautist
Coal miner	Lighthouse keeper	Grocer
Prostitute	Cyclist	Hydraulic engineer
Silversmith	Astronaut	Purser
Hairdresser	Architect	Barber
Locksmith	Blacksmith	Writer
Magician	Soprano	Interviewer
Telephone sanitizer	Air vice-marshal	Laboratory technician
Painter	Film director	Museum curator
Potter	Trainer	
Accountant	Inventor	
Surgeon	Astronomer	

Categories   UNCREATIVE   POSSIBLY CREATIVE   DEFINITELY CREATIVE

Now look again at your "uncreative list". Consider for a moment what "a creative lighthouse keeper" (assuming that was one of your uncreative occupations) would be like. Close your eyes and imagine what he or she would be doing?

Creativity as alternatives

You have just taken the first step towards being creative, which is thinking of *all* the options, not just the obvious ones. The following exercise will test your powers of doing this.

Activity 3: The steel pipe

A steel pipe is embedded vertically in the solid concrete floor of a bare room. The inside diameter of the pipe is 0.06" larger than that of a ping-pong ball (1.50") which rests inside the pipe. You are one of a group of six people in the room. You have:

> 100' of clothes line
> a carpenter's hammer
> a chisel
> a box of weetabix
> a file
> a wire coat hanger
> a monkey wrench
> an egg
> a 60 watt light bulb

How can you get the ball out of the pipe without damaging the pipe, the ball or the floor?

Write your method in the space below.

The censor How many solutions did you find? One very practical solution frequently fails to come up. Suppose I had changed the wording to "you are one of six male members of the group"? Would you then have thought of urinating down the tube? There seems to be a censor in operation when we try to think in a flexible way. Preventing that censor from coming into operation too soon is an important part of being creative.

More is better

But this is not being really creative, since there is only one answer to the problem. What about developing a number of solutions to the same challenge? Here is another problem to which you may think you know "the" answer.

Activity 4: The nine dots problem

Look at the design below.

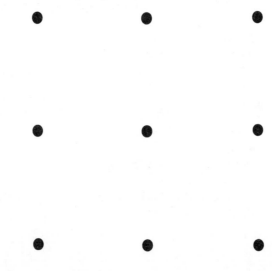

Figure 3

Place a pencil on one of the dots and draw *four* straight lines through all the remaining dots, without lifting the pencil off the paper or retracing your way through any of the lines.

How many *different* ways do you have of doing this?

A common solution to this problem is the following pattern of four lines:

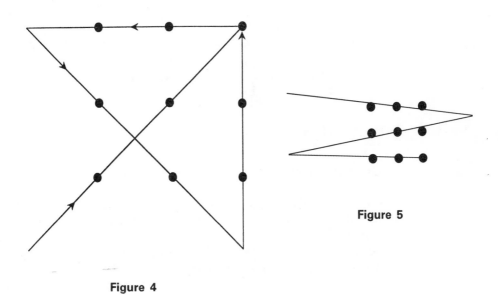

Figure 5

Figure 4

In fact, most people who solve the problem stop at that point. The creative mind will not settle for this but will look for *different* ways of solving the same problem.

Suppose you drew a zig-zag of lines across the page?

Suppose you folded the paper so that the dots touched and then drew one line?

Suppose you cut the dots off the paper and taped them into one length and drew a line through it?

Suppose you cut the dots off the paper and glued them together and stuck the pencil point through them?

Suppose you screwed the paper into a tiny ball and randomly ran the pencil through it until you had touched all nine dots?

Suppose you drew one very thick line with a wallpaper brush?

Suppose you wrote the words "four straight lines" so it touched all the dots?

145

Not stopping at the first answer

These are eight out of 13 solutions that I have seen proffered to the problem. At first they may seem to be "cheating", but this is because they only obey the constraints which really are there rather than those which we surround a problem with. Sebriand is quoted as having written that the chief cause of problems is solutions. I am not sure about that, though I do think the greatest risk to new solutions is old solutions. Several companies have done very well for themselves by going back to look at "second best solutions", the runners up which were rejected at the time because the face validity of one solution seemed so good. When the first solution throws up snags then the second best often proves to have been better after all. But the search for "the" solution prevented it from being properly considered at the time.

What can you vary – attributes

Developing variations on an existing theme is a good way of starting to be more creative. Have you ever noticed how much easier it is to criticise someone else's training, course design or evaluation than to initiate your own? This is partly because there is less of our own sense of value invested in our criticism of others' efforts, and partly because something that is presented to us stimulates all kinds of associations and memories that we would not otherwise have had. The mind works better when it has something to work on. Similarly, recognition is usually better than recall. Which is easier to do – remember 20 words that were presented to us five minutes ago, or pick those 20 out of a list of 40?

Activity 5: Variations on a theme

Take one of the games in this book at random. Read through the brief. Then examine the variations offered on it. Write down as many *new* variations as you can for it.

What did you change? One common way of developing variations to a training game is to take the qualities of the game and vary them systematically one by one. This method of *variation of qualities* can be carried out as follows:

1. List all the qualities of the object or situation. In the case of a training event these might be the number of people working together, whether they are allowed to talk, whether the subject matter is the present moment or not, and whether comments from group members on the activity are exchanged afterwards.
2. Think of as many alternatives as you can to each of these qualities. For the number of people working together this might be single people, pairs, trios, teams (as in relay games) or all the participants together.
3. Draw up a grid showing all the variations possible of all the qualities. For a training game it might look something like this:

Pairs	Alone	Threes	All Teams	Circle	Circle/centre
Talking	Silent	Blindfold	Sign Language		
Past-based	Present-based	Future-based	Timeless		
Comments exchanged	Comments written	Comments acted out	Comments spoken aloud		

The space is for you to add your own qualities and variations.

4. The next stage is to take a random walk through the qualities and imagine what a game would be like if it possessed that combination of qualities.

Activity 6: Systematic variations on a theme

Using the table above, take one entry from each of the rows and use this as the basis for a game. What kind of game will it be. How could it be played? What might its training objectives be?

What can you vary – Objectives

Another way of changing an existing activity is to alter the objective. Many of my own games have developed through me thinking of other objectives that could be met by using an existing game but briefing participants or processing it in a rather different way. I have already indicated in Advantage 15 of using games (p. 7) that the level of processing can be deepened to any number of degrees. Even an energizer could in some circumstances be processed in a way that gives group members a lot of insight into how and why they behaved during the activity.

Activity 7: Themes on a variation

Take a game from this book – *not* the one that you used in Activity 5.

Examine the objectives and compare them to the ones that you are faced with in your own training. Can you think of any other objective which you could meet by playing this game?

What would you have to change about the way that the game was played
What would you have to change about the way that the game is processed?
Would you want to change the name of the game?

What can you vary – Titles

The names that games receive can often be a good hook from which to cluster the aims of the activity. They can often be the starting point, and there have been times when a word or a phrase has been all that is needed to set me off on a new activity. Here are some examples taken from the index to this book.

Activity 8: Re-inventing the wheel

Select *five* of the titles of games from the list below and try to invent from scratch the game that belongs with it. Use the standard headings from this book as guidance – *Title, Summary, Objectives, Materials, Timing, Procedure, Commentary, Variations*. Does it help if you try to sort them out in a different order? In reverse order? Following the list is a pro-forma for you to use for your finished game.

List of games for activity 8

Activity Mime
Amnesia
Appreciative Disagreements
Archaeological Digs
Are you Sitting Comfortably?
Badgering
Backdrops
Blind Walk
Can I Come to the Party?
Chains of Command
Chain Whispers
Circular Reactions
Cockles and Muscles
Confessions of a Trombone Welder
Dress Circle
Extinct Reptiles
Fists
Go-Go
Holy Orders
Invisible Tug-of-War
Just a Minute
Knotty Problems
Listening Limbs
Mind Blowing
Odd Objects
Oxford Circus
Prima Donna
Reinventing the Wheel
Siamese Triplets
Telephone Kiosks
Trillions
Truth Option
What are *you* Doing?

A Gender Setting
Amorous Andy
Bandstand
A's and B's
Babel
Battle of the Sexes
Bagels
Bunker
Catflap
Chain Mime
Chorus Line
Class of their Own
Cocktail Party
Continuum
Elementary
Exotic Fruits
Fruit Salad
Groundnuts
Icebergs
Jacket Potatoes
Just a Minute
Legover
Martians
Number Crunches
Off the Top
Paganini
Problems without Words
RSVP
Spaghetti Junction
Towel Rack
True Stories
Ugly Sisters
What would You Do?

Proforma for Activity 8

Title

Summary

Objectives

Materials

Timing

Procedure

Commentary

Variations

Actually I was a little deceptive here. About a third of the titles given here are ones for which I have never invented a training game! I would be interested to know what you have invented.

A kickstart – Simile

Another way of giving your mind a "kickstart" and to help you to develop new and original approaches is to compare your client group with other things. This may have already occurred to you in your more desperate moments! If not, try the following exercise.

Activity 9: Cheese sandwich

Consider, the way you did in Activity 2, the meaningfulness of the following comparisons that can be made. To what extent are they true for you? To the extent that they are true, what hints do they give you on how to approach your clients, and what kind of training game you might offer them? Suppose they *were* in that category?

My client group are like

> ants
> zombies
> bricks
> statues
> books
> fruits
> cakes
> the decor of houses
> a board game
> cartoon characters
> a machine
> a giant animal
> a recipe
> a cheese sandwich

What similes of your own can you add?

Some more kickstarts

The literature of creativity shows that dreams and fantasies are often the starting point for many important discoveries (such as the benzine ring) or creative works (Coleridge's *Kubla Khan*). I am not sure if training games count as discoveries or works of art, but I am sure

151

that the same principles apply. Jokes, images, stories, advertisements or anything else to which you are receptive enough can stimulate a train of thought. What makes one person more creative than another is perhaps the ability to seize on that and develop it.

Helps and hindrances to creativity

Having, I hope, started being more creative in your approach to games, you can think about what makes the practice harder and easier for yourself.

Activity 10: Helps and hindrances

Think over times when you have been or failed to be creative when it was important that you produced an idea of your own, or you had a particular problem to wrestle with. What features of the situation, what external factors made it particularly easy and particularly hard for you to be creative in that situation? I have put down some of my own to start you off:

Things that helped	*Things that hindered*
Talking to self	Fear of taking risks
Doodling	Inconvenience
Telling a story	Interruption
Brainstorming	Loss of face
Imagery	Lack of time
Be the problem	
Think of something irrelevant	

Once you come to understand your own creative stimulants and your own difficulties then you will be able to plan many of them out. This is the point where perhaps you need to put the book down and brainstorm with a colleague.

Concluding reflection

My experience is that the best way to develop creativity is to discover how to practice it and forget any theory you have learned. The most helpful book on becoming creative that I have discovered is Adams (1974), which contains an excellent Reader's Guide for anyone who wishes to explore the subject further. Adams gives some useful hints on developing different languages (images, mathematics, verbal, conceptual) to tackle problems in the most appropriate way. Some of this is developed in Adams (1986). Eitington (1989) has attempted to apply some of these principles specifically to training.

The other key to creativity is the time management principle that if you are going to do anything – including being creative – then you must make time for it. When most people thing about creativity they do so in more or less the terms of Shelley's famous image (Shelley (1988):

> "the mind in creation is as a fading coal, which some invisible influence, like an inconstant wind, awakens to transitory brightness . . . the conscious portions of our natures are unprophetic of either its approach or its departure."

In fact we have a great capacity to develop The Mind In Creation at will, and one essential is to put aside the time. Even setting the clock 15 minutes before you need to awaken can help. Mental muscles, like physical ones, also become stronger and more supple the more that they are used. The mistake that many people make is to try and be creative when they are tired. Like any form of mental effort, this is doomed to failure. The first ten games that I invented were the hardest. After that I found that the process began to happen automatically.

Please note that all the games listed in the Objectives Index under Problem Solving or Creativity can be harnessed to the invention of new games.

References

Adair, John (1983) *Effective Leadership*, Gower.

Adams, James L. (1974) *Conceptual Blockbusting, A Guide To Better Ideas*, Penguin.

Adams, James L. (1986) *The Care and Feeding of Ideas*, Penguin.

Anastasi, Anne (1979) *Fields of Applied Psychology*, McGraw Hill.

Bank, John (ed.) (1990) *A Guide to Best Practice for Development Training in the Outdoors*, Development Training Users' Trust, Cranfield School of Management, Bedford.

Bartlett, F. C. (1932) *Remembering, A study in experimental and social psychology*, Cambridge University Press.

Belbin, R. M. (1981) *Management Teams*, Heinemann.

Benson, Jarlath (1987) *Working more creatively with groups*, Tavistock, London.

Beresford-Cooke, Carole (1984) *The Book of Massage*, Ebury Press.

Bond, Tim (1988) *Games for Social and Life Skills*, Hutchinson

Brandes, D. (1982) *Gamesters' Handbook Two*, Hutchinson.

Brandes, D. and Phillips, D. (1978) *Gamesters' Handbook*, Hutchinson.

Bryan, J. and Test, M. "Models and helping: naturalistic studies in aiding behaviour", *Journal of Personality and Social Psychology*, VI: 400–07.

Bryson, Bill (1990) *Dictionary of Troublesome Words (2nd edition)*, Penguin.

Clark, Neil and Fraser, Tony (1987) *The Gestalt Approach, an introduction for managers and trainers*, Roffey Park, Horsham.

Clark, N., Phillips K. and Barker, D. (1984) *Unfinished Business*, Gower.

Clinard, Helen (1985) *Winning ways to succeed with people*, Gulf.

Dainow, Sheila and Bailey, Caroline (1988) *Developing Skills With People*, Wiley.

Egan, Gerard (1986) *The Skilled Helper*, Brooks/Cole.

Elgood, Chris (1985) *Handbook of Management Training Games (4th edition)*, Gower.

Eitington, J. E. (1989) *The Winning Trainer*, Gulf.

Freud, A. (1936) *The Ego and the Mechanisms of Defence*, Hogarth Press.

Gessell, A. (1946) *The Child from Five to Ten*, Harper.

Hampden-Turner, Charles (1981) *Maps of the Mind*, Mitchell Beazley.

Handy, Charles B. (1985) *Understanding Organisations (3rd edition)*, Penguin.

Hargie, Owen (1986) *Handbook of Communication Studies*, Routledge.

Honey, Peter and Mumford, Alan (1986) *The Manual of Learning Styles*, Peter Honey.

Hopkins, J. (1981) "Seeing yourself as others see you", *Social Work Today*, 12 (25): 10–13.

Institute of Personnel Management (1984) *Continuous Development: People at Work*.

Kolb, D. A. (1984) *Experiential Learning*, Prentice Hall.

Laird, Dugan (1985) *Approaches to Training and Development*, Addison Wesley.

Lefkowitz, M., Blake, R. and Moulton, J. (1955) "Status factors in pedestrian violation of traffic signals", *Journal of Abnormal and Social Psychology* 51: 704–6.

Lloyd, Peter and Mayes, Andrew (1984) *Introduction to Psychology: An Integrated Approach*, Fontana.

Loftus, E. F. (1979) *Eyewitness testimony*, Harvard University Press.

Margerison, Charles and McCann, Dick (1990) *Team Management*, Mercury.

Maxwell-Hudson, Clare (1988) *The Complete Book of Massage*, Dorling Kindersley.

Newstrom, John A. and Scannell, Edward E. (1980) *Games Trainers Play*, McGraw-Hill.

Noon, James (1985) *'A' Time*, Chapman and Hall.

Opie, I. and Opie, P. (1969) *Children's Games in Street and Playground*, Oxford University Press.

Parker, Dorothy (1973) *The Collected Dorothy Parker*, Penguin.

Pfeiffer, J. W. (1973) "Risk Taking", in Pfeiffer, J. W. and Jones, J. E. *The 1973 Annual Handbook for Group Facilitators*, University Associates (pp. 124–6).

Pfeiffer, J. W. and Jones, J. E. (1972) "Openness, collusion and feedback", in Pfeiffer, J. W. and Jones, J. E. *The 1972 Annual Handbook for Group Facilitators*, University Associates (pp. 197–201).

Pfeiffer, J. W. and Jones, J. E. (1974–83) *A Handbook of Structured Experiences for Human Relations Training*, Volumes 1–9, University Associates.

Rackham, N. (1977) *Behaviour Analysis in Training*, McGraw Hill.

Rakos, Richard R. (1986) *Asserting and Confronting*, in Hargie, O. *Handbook of Communication Studies*, Routledge.

Remocker, Jane A. and Storch, Elizabeth T. (1979) *Action Speaks Louder*, Churchill Livingstone.

Ribeaux, Peter and Poppleton, Stephen (1978) *Psychology and Work*, Macmillan.

Rogers, Jenny (1989) *Adults Learning*, Open University Press, London.

Rogers, Carl R. (1951) *Client Centre Therapy*, Houghton-Mifflin, Boston.

Shelley, P. B. (1988) "A defence of poetry", in D. L. Clark (ed.) *Shelley's Prose*, Fourth Estate.

Stammers, Robert and Patrick, John (1975) *Psychology Training*, Methuen.

Stewart, I. and Joines, V. (1987) *TA Today*, Lifespace.

Swenson, C. H. (1983) *Introduction to Interpersonal Relations*, Scott Foresman.

Van Ments, Morry (1989) *Effective Use of Role Play*, Kogan Page.

Index of games by objectives